40 Meditations

Stories Inspired by Yoga and Practices For Transformation

By

Robin D. Bruce

Illuminated Notions, Austin, Texas

Paperback ISBN: 978-0-9963728-2-4

eBook ISBN: 978-0-9963728-3-1

Library of Congress Control Number: 2015952252

40 Meditations

by Robin D. Bruce

Published by Illuminated Notions, Austin, Texas, 2015

http://www.yogasong.org

A big thank you to all the healers, teachers, mentors, spirit seeking brothers and sisters! Thank you to Russell Eric Dobda, Liz Brown, Nata Polyushkevich Nikketa Burgess, my grandmother and grandfather Carolyn and Gary Bruce, and my mother Tamilyn Dupaquier.

Table of Contents

Introduction

When I first began practicing Kundalini Yoga in 2002, I didn't know how deeply an unassuming, weekly yoga class would influence my life. But the alchemy that took place in the back room of San Antonio's Witte Museum created a foundation for me to foster habits of discipline, self-love, and commitment. In the decade following, this magical practice has taken me across the Atlantic Ocean and also within, into the private spaces of my heart. It's even nurtured my creativity and ushered in new experiences with different styles of yoga and meditation. But I keep coming back home to Kundalini Yoga.

"It takes 40 days to break a habit," Yogi Bhajan, teacher of Kundalini Yoga in the West always said. I remember my first 40-day meditation experience. I committed to a daily practice of "Kriya for the 10 bodies." I woke up at 4am before my early morning shift at the coffee shop to breathe and move. As a gentle 20-year old, I thought that after 40 days, I would be done and all problems solved through my 40-day commitment. But in spiritual practice, we are never done. We practice everyday to keep energy moving, to keep stagnation from settling in.

There are many ways to approach a meditation practice. For beginners, it's best to try several methods of meditation and when you find one that deeply resonates with you – it moves you – it inspires tears, reflection and progress over obstacles, then commit to a 40-day practice with that one meditation.

A 40-day practice consists of 40 consecutive days with the same meditation. This book provides many meditations that are great for beginners and long-time practitioners looking for a refresher. Thank you so much for your interest and desire to heal, transform, and connect to yourself.

How To Use This Book

Note the meditations that bring up the most resistance or make you feel at peace. Practice these meditations for longer than a day until you feel like you are ready to move on to another meditation. If a meditation is particularly powerful for you, practice it everyday for 40 consecutive days for a strong transformational experience.

Each lesson follows with a journaling exercise. Writing allows you to process and integrate the meditations. I recommend getting a sixty to eighty page journal dedicated to this book to record your reflections and experiences throughout the course.

When you're asked to free-write, see how long you can write or type without thinking or allowing the pen to leave the paper. Think of journaling as a cognitive brain-dump where there is no judgment. After you write, leave your writings be. Don't go back and read them until the end of your 40 days unless otherwise specified in the journaling exercise.

Meditation Environment

Find a place in your home or in nature that you can return to daily. Allow this to be a place of sanctuary where you feel supported, safe and loved. I suggest building a personal altar with fresh flowers, photos of loved ones, and words of inspiration.

Here is a basic method for creating your own altar. Set up a small table that is about eye level and adorn it with candles, pictures, written intentions, stones, trinkets and crystals that hold personal meaning for you. It's fun to be creative and child-like when crafting this altar because your essence is that of a playful child.

It's also important that your space is clear of certain types of energy. For instance, you wouldn't want to practice yoga or meditate in an area where people are consuming alcohol, smoking or watching television. You want your meditative space to be neutral, free from external energy. Even if this is the corner of your bedroom, adorn it so beautifully that it will be an inviting space that you'll want to return to everyday.

Props

The yoga and meditation practices included in this book require minimal props like meditation cushions or blocks. When you sit in meditation, the idea is to be as comfortable as possible. When you sit upright and cross-legged, ideally your knees are located below your hips. If not, then sit on a blanket or pillow so that the knees are below the hips. If your upper back begins to bother you, then lie flat on the floor. Some meditation teachers do not suggest this because students often fall asleep, and the discomfort when sitting is actually part of the meditation.

However, there is a point when sitting upright becomes distracting and can deter a beginner practitioner from practicing at all. If you are in this category, lie on your back. Also, if you are under the weather, have physical ailments, or are very pregnant, give yourself permission to relax and lie down.

Wear clothing that feels good on your skin and allows you to sit and move comfortably. Simple cotton clothing that feels loose on the skin is good for meditation.

Some of the meditations ask that you set a timer. You can use a basic stopwatch or a timer on your phone. I recommend the Insight Timer app available for download on your iPhone or android. It allows you to set minute intervals and sounds as a relaxing chime at the end of your meditation.

Kundalini Meditations

You will notice that some of the meditations will have an asterisk and the word Kundalini. This denotes that the meditation is a Kundalini meditation and the ritual aspects of the Kundalini practice are observed. In the Kundalini practice, we tune in with the mantra 'Ong Namo Guru Dev Namo' three times and then practice our meditation. Once the meditation is complete, we tune out by chanting the mantra 'Sat Nam' three times. You will also notice that some meditations suggest music accompaniment. For these meditations, refer to the resources section.

Day 1: Slow Down and Listen

Yoga teaches me to befriend my body

When I was faced with a life-altering illness, I had no idea that I was being handed a gift. I began practicing yoga in 2002 at the age of twenty, when my body, mind and spirit were broken. My lower back constantly ached and I had frequent grand mal seizures that inhibited me from driving or keeping a regular job. The seizures were no joke. One moment I'd be at lunch with friends and the next moment on the floor thrashing about, my tense body struggling for air. Each time I woke up feeling disappointed in myself, "I had another one didn't I?" I would ask. I also woke up in pain, feeling like I'd been in a biker brawl, with a swollen jaw and bruised eye as evidence of my private fight.

With the experience of illness so young came the thought that I would be limited for the rest of my life. This scared the shit out of me. So I made my first grown-up decision: I gave myself the power to make changes in my lifestyle habits – the one thing I could control. I changed what I ate, began exercising regularly, went to bed early, supplemented my diet with vitamins, and began attending yoga classes. These classes proved to be game-changers.

Attending yoga classes helped me tune into my body sensations, developing a kinder relationship with myself. Before the back injury I played competitive basketball and viewed my body as a machine, something I controlled with my thoughts. My regular yoga practice changed that view and helped me embrace my body like a friend, a valuable sensory information tool aiding my thought and decision processes. The experience of my body informing my mind and not the other way around helped repair my nervous system. The healing came about slowly, but it did come. I learned to listen to the messages from my body – when to rest, when to sleep, what to eat - all of this intercommunication the result of a regular yoga and meditation practice. The seizures subsided and the pain in my back dissipated. There was more inner work to be done, but I was able to get back to life again with greater appreciation for the simple pleasures – and enthusiasm to try new ones! I began to take guitar classes at our local junior college, got a part-time barista job, and was able to finally drive again.

In this way injury and limitation can be precious gifts. They force us to stop everything so we can learn, experience, and be with ourselves.

Meditation

Set a timer for 5 minutes. Lie down on your back. Inhale and exhale through your nose. Feel the natural rhythm of your breath. Then, mentally repeat the following affirmation noticing any reaction or resistance.

Affirmation: "My body's natural state is wellness. When I feel unwell, I receive that information as a call to slow down, release and remember to care of myself."

Any variation of this affirmation will do, as long as the idea remains the same: Our bodies want to be well, and when we are unwell, it's a reminder to slow down and nurture ourselves. Once you repeat the affirmation mentally a few times, notice how you feel.

Journal Exercise

1. Free write two pages directly after the meditation. Write about any openings or resistances that came to the surface during the meditation.

2. Fill in the blank with all the words that come to mind:

   a. When I slow down I feel _____.

   b. I only feel like it's okay to relax under these conditions: _____.

   c. List three ways you can care for yourself when you're feeling unwell.

Day 2: Patience Pays

Yoga teaches me I can do shit I never thought I could do

Sweat driving channels down my forehead, hips forward, chest lifted, head relaxed back – I find myself in full camel pose. Without any forcing or pushing, I reach back and my heels are there. I arrive in it. With a history of low back pain coupled with a movement philosophy of taking it easy and slow, the fact that I arrive in a deep backbend is remarkable.

I've often joked about myself as the lazy yogi, opting for restorative, gentle, and restful classes over vinyasa. I'd much rather meditate and chant than sweat. A recent exchange with a student reflected my personal preference.

"I have low back pain, but I think it's important to stay fit so I do cross fit and run five miles a day. What do you do?" asked the student.

"I do breathing exercises, chant, and walk," I replied.

I love my body and I want it to work for a long time. My days as an athlete punishing it, squeezing it, weighting it and trying to force it into shapes are over. Hiking is ample cardio for now and I'm happy with my shape. Sometimes I wonder if being happy with myself is part of why I stay healthy.

When my body decided it wanted to go into full camel pose I was surprised, because I hadn't been physically working toward it. I have been working toward being more open, accepting, and vulnerable. In this case, the emotional informed the physical.

The point is, I arrived in a posture; and that one time felt so special, like a gift. I didn't force it and I felt so good being there - heart open with ease.

Meditation

Set your timer for 3-5 minutes. Lie on your back and bring the soles of your feet together and separate the knees for supta baddha konasana. To create more comfort, you may tuck a small blanket underneath each thigh.

Direct your mind toward a goal or intention you've been working toward. Mentally vibrate the word "soften" when focusing on your goal. This is giving your body and mind permission to relax, knowing that the mental intention and daily action is enough. You will eventually arrive. Keep reminding yourself to soften until the timer sounds.

Journal Exercise

Sometimes we work hard instead of working smart. It's a paradox that we can often accomplish more when we slow down and direct our intention toward one thing. We require constant reminding that we are enough in this moment, and that our goals are best realized in the spirit of love not competition. Our daily actions toward that goal will lead us to arrive.

1. Choose three of the following affirmations. Write each of the chosen affirmations ten times.

    I am enough in this moment.

    I am validated in this moment regardless of my actions.

    When I soften, my intentions are realized.

    When I allow myself to work with grace and ease, my intentions are realized.

    The most important goal is that I love myself here and now.

2. Write 1-2 pages about the affirmations you chose, noting if you feel any resistance or resonance with them and why.

Day 3: Do What You Love Right Now

Yoga helps me to see that I am self-validated

Permission is defined as consent, especially formal consent. After teaching yoga for many years, the word permission crept into my vocabulary and I said it often, "give yourself permission to bend your knees." Where had that concept come from, and how had it become so glaring in my personal life that it leaked into class? It came from a personal declaration that I am self-validated and consequently granted permission to feel and experience.

I used to wait around for someone else to tell me that I was good enough or ready to pursue a personal goal or dream. In many areas of my life, I was waiting for a stamp, certificate, degree or certification permitting me to move forward. But the most important "program" I studied was one in which I sat with myself everyday in meditation. This solitary practice helped me to see that I am the one who chooses when to move forward with my dreams and projects. I have the power to validate myself.

It's with this sentiment that I decided I was good enough to record my first album in 2011, *Blissful Sadhana*. It was an intimidating process. I mean hearing myself on a voicemail was tough enough, but a whole hour of my singing voice...yikes! Yet, I felt supported by my practice and a deep connection to the voice within that said, "It's time."

If you are wondering whether you're ready or good enough to do the thing that you love, I'm here to say that you are! There is someone right now longing for that special thing you have to offer.

Meditation

Part of self-validation comes from connecting to your wholeness. That is, realizing that you don't need something from the outside to verify that you are ready. Connecting with your wholeness means that you have all that you need inside of you in this moment.

Set your timer for 3-11 minutes. Sit in a comfortable posture, lying on the back if you need to.

Begin to breathe slowly and consciously, noticing your inhale and exhale. Then, begin to mentally practice this mantra:

inhale: mentally say "I am"
exhale: mentally say "Whole"

inhale: mentally say "I am"
exhale: mentally say "Complete"

inhale: mentally say "I am"
exhale: mentally say "I am"

Cycle through the mantra until the timer sounds. Rest silently for a few moments, meditating on your wholeness.

Journal Exercise

So many times I've held myself back from completing a project because I didn't feel like it was perfect enough. So often we allow perfection to get in the way of progress. The journaling exercise this week helps us embrace the imperfections, so that we can move forward toward completion.

1. Write about a time when you felt imperfect and were judged for your imperfections.

2. Write a letter to yourself from the perspective of an adult to the younger you. Soothe yourself with kind words and express how proud you are of "younger you" for finishing something. I mean, what an accomplishment to put your feelings, creations, and self out there!

Day 4: Take the Leap

Yoga teaches me I can do shit I never thought I could do - part b

In 2005 a friend of mine asked, "If you could do one thing in life what would it be?" I responded sheepishly that I would like to record a studio album one day. I also expressed the silly dream of singing with a live band. I didn't know that both dreams were soon to be realized.

My move to San Marcos, Texas placed me strategically in a bursting live music scene filled with good spirited, talented bands. I jammed with a few people, but nothing much materialized. After a few years of focused attention on my mantra practice, I heard about a band that was looking for a singer. By their name I knew I wanted to be their next singer. The name was Jamiroqueen – a Jamiroquai tribute band.

I was introduced to Jamiroquai's music at the age of fourteen. I heard a mix of rebellion, anger, happiness, joy and the power of faith in light disco pulses. Just the thought of honoring Jamiroquai by singing their songs made my heart smile.

I was nervous to audition because I hadn't ever fronted a six-piece band before. Though inexperienced and apprehensive, I knew from my yoga and meditation practice that anxiety is temporary and smaller than the promise of a new experience. I allowed the group to see who I was by putting myself out there a hundred percent. They dug it and asked me to join the band.

Singing with this group is so special. Each member is precious and unique, and it's a gift to share space together. At one show, as I belted out Rick James' "Give It to Me Baby," a couple of horn players randomly joined us onstage and my heart skipped a beat! Eight musicians playing together as one, a dream realized; and my yoga practice helped me take the leap. I put myself out there and received a priceless experience.

Meditation

The focus of this meditation is on the temporary nature of sensations. We often allow our thoughts, emotions and nerves get the best of us, keeping us away from new experiences. This meditation helps you develop a relationship with those temporary sensations and the consequent ability to let them pass without freaking you out.

Set your timer for 12 minutes. Use four separate three-minute intervals, with the alarm sounding every three minutes. Read through the following meditation before practicing.

Step 1: For the first three minutes sit and notice your thoughts. What kind of thoughts have you been having? What's the pace of your thoughts? Have they been light or heavy in nature? Has there been a particular topic you've been chewing on?

Step 2: For the next three minutes notice your emotions. Do any particular emotions emerge in relationship to your thought cycles? As emotions emerge, welcome them, even the unpleasant ones. For instance, if you are feeling insecurity, don't push it away. Welcome it in, like you would a houseguest, projecting love and kindness to it. For example you might say, "Hey disappointment! I haven't seen you in a while! Where did you come from?" Investigate your emotions in this way, one by one.

Step 3: For the next three minutes notice your body. In particular, notice the prevailing emotion and where you feel it in your body. Notice parts of your body that might feel discomfort or ease, hot or cold, heaviness or lightness. Just notice.

Step 4: For the final three minutes, each time you inhale, breathe in the uncomfortable sensation that came up during the meditation. If nothing came up, then focus on a person or circumstance that you feel needs love and healing. On the inhale focus on the sensation, circumstance, or person, drawing in awareness of pain and suffering. In a sense, you are inhaling empathy. On the exhale send unconditional love and kindness to the person, circumstance or sensation.

For example: Inhale awareness of the pain from rejection. Exhale kindness, joy and love to yourself and all the other people who have ever felt the pain of rejection.

The final step is the practice of transforming suffering into fuel for kindness and joy. We often make choices in our lives to shield ourselves from discomfort and pain. This practice does the opposite. It acknowledges those things we'd like to hide or push away and showers them with love. It also unites us with everyone else who has experienced this same discomfort, so that we do not feel alone.

Journal Exercise

Free write 1-2 pages in response to the following questions:

What do I do when I feel reactive? For example, when I experience conflict with a friend or I'm about to do something outside of my comfort zone, what is my usual action? Would my reaction be different if I waited until the emotional component passed? What might that look or feel like?

Day 5: The Journey is the Goal

Yoga teaches me to be process-oriented

I can get wrapped up in a goal. Sometimes, I forget to have fun along the way and treasure each step on the journey. When I hyper-focus, all of my actions become a means by which I work toward an end. But, does that mean that this moment is empty if it's not being used to work toward a goal? Of course not! This moment is the goal - it's the most important moment of my life! Yoga teaches me to recognize the value of process. By treating an action as an end instead of a means to get somewhere else, I can embrace the value of each moment as whole and complete. Then I have space to make small choices that lead toward an intention.

I remember my journey toward college graduation. The first of my family to attend college, I thought that upon graduation, all would fall into place and the universe would magically unfold somehow and grant me ultimate happiness and stability.

The reality was quite different. After graduation I was more miserable and lost than ever, and here's why: I had raced through my degree plan, basing my happiness on future graduation. I missed precious opportunities to make connections and have experiences along the pathway to my goal. I was so busy preparing for my internship that I didn't take the time to be, or be real with myself and affirm that I was on the right path - in alignment with my whole self.

As a yoga teacher now, many people ask for help losing weight, working toward a yoga posture, or achieving some other goal. Yes, yoga can do that, but if we start with an idea or picture of what the end looks like, then we don't allow for the picture to change into something more aligned with who we are deep inside. We can also miss the opportunity to experience the magic inherent in the transformation process itself.

It's better to set a goal as an idea or "intention." That's why we set an intention in the beginning of class rather than a goal. We focus on an idea or image that we intend to occur, and allow the fruition of that idea to take shape in a natural way that is more magical than we could ever imagine. I'm still learning this lesson, and I experience it as a process forever unfolding in waves of humility and understanding.

Meditation

One of the habits of our mind is to think that another place is better than the one we're in at this moment. For example, you might say, "When I get that new job, then I'll be happy or satisfied." Well, why not decide to be satisfied now? Why make your happiness conditional? Chances are, when you get that new job you'll find new ways to be dissatisfied. Maybe you won't make enough money or will have to learn a new skill set. Then the mind shifts again to another place other than where you're currently at, where life is better.

A powerful skill set is to consolidate your energy by being present and aware. This place where you are right now is valuable and special because it is this moment. When we connect to the breath and body through yoga and meditation, we are reminded of the simple majesty of being human and alive, here and now!

Step 1: Sit comfortably with the hands on the knees. Breathe in and out through your nose. On the inhale, lengthen through your spine and draw your chest forward through the columns of your arms and lift the chin a tad. On the exhale, roll your spine back and draw the chin in toward the neck.

Do this movement very slowly so that the length of your breath matches the length of your movement. Repeat four or five cycles of inhale and exhale.

Step 2: Set your timer for 3 minutes and place your thumb on your wrist until you feel your pulse. Meditate on your heart's rhythm. Take into your being the idea that you can feel your heart working for you. Right now your heart is pumping energy to your extremities so that you can live and enjoy this moment. Take in your humanity and how special your body is – how special you are.

Journal Exercise

The idea behind this lesson is that we always want to be somewhere we're not, doing something else other than what we're doing because that other thing is better than what's happening in the present moment.

In your journal today write one page completely in the present moment. For example: "I am here sitting at my laptop and noticing the soft breath underneath my nose." Notice how often you want to talk about the past or the future, and if you do, don't judge yourself for it. Gently guide your pen and mind to the present sensation. This will bring awareness to how often we focus our attention on the past and the future.

Day 6: It's Okay To Feel

Yoga teaches me to experience my emotions

One of my favorite sayings is, "Emotion is good. It's energy in motion. It means things are moving." The tricky part is when we become identified with our emotions. We might say, "I am sad," or "I am angry," when we really mean "I am experiencing sadness," or "I am experiencing anger."

I love this concept because it lets me experience the emotion without identifying myself as the emotion. It also removes the shame around experiencing emotion. At one time I had an idea of the perfect yogi, always blissed-out, either at peace or extremely happy. Conversely inherent in the perfect yogi view is that the experience and expression of emotion shows weakness.

With that image in my mind, I couldn't ever live up to the perfect meditator I'd placed on a pedestal. Also, sometimes I noticed students in my class projecting me to a place "higher" than themselves, even higher than me. That was an uncomfortable place to be because it did not feel authentic. I honor my highest Self, yet am wonderfully human in the same space.

There is union between the feminine and the masculine when we allow ourselves permission to feel our feelings and recognize that these feelings are temporary and do not define us. When I feel something, I don't block it. I allow it to pass through, knowing that it will change with time. This feels right to me, though I find myself becoming judgmental as emotions pass through, saying things like "I shouldn't be feeling this. Everything should be manageable all the time." or "How did I let someone make me feel this way?"

It's silly to judge ourselves for our emotions; or to blame others for them. By denying emotions, we give them more power as they linger, waiting to be expressed. So, allow yourself to feel and experience your emotions. Your feelings are cues as to what is right and in alignment for you and what no longer fits. When you allow them to pass through without acting on them, they often lose their power, their hold on you. They also provide valuable information in the process.

Meditation

This meditation requires that you listen to ocean sounds. You can find the music in the Resources Section.

Set your timer for 7 minutes. Lie on your back and listen to the sound of the ocean waves.

Imagine the waves traveling from the crown of your head down to the toes. Then, back from the toes to the crown of the head. Feel the energy of the waves moving up and down through the body.

Invite your body to soften and relax as you allow the waves to move through you without attaching any description to the sensation.

This is the wave movement of emotion. The next time you feel strong emotion, embrace the feeling and let it move through you like a wave without managing, judging or controlling it. Give it space to move around and experience it.

Journal Exercise

1. Write about a time when you felt a certain way, yet negated your own emotion. What did that feel like to deny your feelings? What were the circumstances around it? Were you not in a place where you were allowed to feel?

2. Write a letter to yourself in the past. Tell yourself that it's okay to feel and that you are learning how to allow emotion to pass through you like a wave. Offer words of sincerity and encouragement to that part of yourself who was made to feel like it's not okay to be yourself.

Day 7: Do Nice Things For Yourself

Yoga teaches me to go easy on myself

"Treating myself like a precious object makes me stronger." I read this quote in Julie Cameron's *The Artist's Way* in 2011 and it resonates with me still today. Yoga teaches me the importance of self-care. Adequate rest, baths with scented oils, massages, time alone, long walks with good company - these items aren't optional, they're necessary. Treating myself well, like a precious gift, allows me to have a greater capacity to teach and heal. When we treat ourselves well, we are able to be more present as lovers, parents, siblings, and friends.

We can be too hard on ourselves; and the world is tough enough as it is without our own strong inner criticisms. When I start to get into a critical thought cycle, I go back to the quote by Julie and do something nice for myself.

Meditation

Today our meditation takes us away from our altars and cushions. Today's meditation is to do something nice for your Self. Some ideas: Take a warm bath with salts and scented oils, paint your toenails, go for a walk in nature, watch a funny movie, roll around on the carpet, anything that feels like a treat, do it! Give yourself permission to enjoy.

Journal Exercise

Make a list of twenty or more actions that feel like a treat. Choose items that make you feel precious and content. When you begin to close down and be hard on yourself, go to this list and treat yourself with one of these actions. If you've always wanted to climb an indoor wall, have that listed and ready for the next time you're looking for a treat!

Day 8: It's Okay To Ask For Help

Yoga teaches me to ask for and accept help

I once had the attitude that I could do it all by myself. Actually, that was my preferred method of doing things. That way, I felt like I didn't have to depend on anyone else but myself. But life has a way of teaching us lessons and life delivered circumstances in which I had to ask for and receive help - frequently.

The big financial face slap came after the divorce. Doing life without a partner meant working most waking hours and still barely making rent. My heart couldn't bear another month of financial uncertainty. I prayed vehemently for support! And then the help came in the most beautiful and unpredictable ways:

The student who gave me a hundred dollar bill wrapped neatly in an envelope after class. The garden fresh strawberries delivered to me by my neighbor, unasked for, at my door. The invitation to dinner that provided food and comfort when I really needed it. The sublet apartment opportunity that appeared at just the right time. The food co-op that fed me all summer. The job at Wake the Dead Coffee House that started just when I got into my new apartment. The local teaching opportunity at Red Dawg Hot Yoga that allowed me to share what I love to do with the local community.

And not to mention the emotional support from my friends and family: The long talks with my mother when she said so wisely "You're just in a transition right now." The conversations with my longest, best girlfriend that kept me grounded when I was at my most raw and vulnerable.

Receiving help was uncomfortable at first. I beat myself up a lot. I wondered why I'd put myself in a situation where I had to rely on others to get through a challenging time. But now that the dust has settled, I see that accepting help and allowing myself to be seen at my most vulnerable created support structures that I still rely on today.

Accepting help isn't a sign of weakness; it's a sign of strength. To openly admit that there are circumstances beyond my control and ability to fix is a beautiful human quality. And because of experiencing the reliance on others, I feel stronger than ever before because I am a product of everyone's charity and love.

Meditation

This is called the cosmic hug meditation. It's cosmic because it asks you to imagine yourself hugging and being hugged by someone on the other side of the planet, and finally all the beings on this earth, right here and right now.

Sit at your altar and set your timer anywhere from 3-11 minutes. Light a candle. Sit with your eyes open, staring at the blue part of the flame. Imagine one person on the other side of the planet who is in need of a hug, love, support, and encouragement.

Imagine yourself hugging that person. Fully embrace them and send them love. Then imagine all the humans on this planet hugging each other simultaneously, all at once feeling the joy of each other, the warmth through the struggle that we all feel. Hug and be hugged by the whole planet.

Journal Exercise

This journal exercise opens you to ask for and receive help.

We all are working on something in our personal lives. Whether it be connection to others, communication or financial stability, we all know our Achilles' heel. In this exercise, sincerely ask for help resolving your stuff. Your entry may read something like "Dear energy of love, the energy of the universe, I am having a difficult time sharing my feelings lately. Could you help me with that? I am open to receiving help in these specific ways, but also in ways that I can't see."

Write one page around each topic you wish to see moved, illuminated and transformed, asking for specific or open-ended help.

Day 9: You Don't Have To Suffer To Get Results

Yoga teaches me to slow down, breathe, and find pleasure in my daily activities

I used to be a stressed-out yoga teacher – a walking contradiction. When I attended yoga classes, I thought relaxation was something I got to feel after I did the work of asana. I walked into class wound up and besides the brief relaxation at the end, I left pretty wound up. But one day that changed when a teacher gave our class permission to slow down, link breath with movement and find ease while in a pose. I felt a deep ahhhhh sensation in my hips, shoulders and heart. This cue not only revolutionized the way I practice yoga but also affected the way I move through life – with more ease.

A traditional yoga class focuses on the balance of sukha and sthira, effort and ease. I cultivated the effort part and figured the ease would come after I worked hard enough in a pose. This is how I viewed life for much of my thirty years here on earth. If I just worked hard enough, then life would surely become easy, after the hard work part.

Not to diminish the respectable quality of working hard, but why don't we equally honor the quality of finding ease? I love having easeful people in my life, reminding me to be present, eat a cookie and smile. And slowly, I've become one myself!

I live in a college town, so I frequently hear conversations about degree plans and consequent life trajectory. Before yoga class, a student asked me what type of degree I had.

"Nutrition," I replied.

"What are you going to do with it?" she asked.

"This is my job." I said. "I'm doing it." I'm here now. I'm not on my way to something else. I love what I'm doing. This is my ease.

I wish I had known and practiced this while in college. I tended to focus on the suffering caused by this assignment or that project rather than find ease and comfort somewhere in the university, slowing down and breathing long enough to realize the beauty of being alive.

Luckily I have the chance to be present now and so do you. Find the ease now and let go of the work and reward model of thinking. Sometimes we can skip right to the reward, easy peasy.

Meditation

The idea that life has to be hard is something that was engrained in us by the world around us. Our parents encouraged this idea to prepare us for what life would bring, not knowing that by thinking this way we bring more of the same toward us like a magnet, drawing in the energy of suffering, heaviness and toil of hard work. This meditation asks you to release any heaviness you feel in your day-to-day and choose love as your pathway to ease.

Set your timer for 11 minutes. Lie on your back and for the first few minutes notice the flow of your breath. Notice where you might be tensing, holding, or forcing your breath. Keep paying close attention to your breath until it starts to flow effortlessly in and out without any resistance. Don't be concerned if it takes the whole eleven minutes to find a non-resistant breath.

Once you find a flow with your breath, repeat the following mantra out loud three times, then silently until the timer sounds. All the while focus on the non-resistant flow of your breath.

Mantra: "Love is the path of ease. I love myself and offer all my worries to the energy of love."

Journal Exercise

1. Write down all the words that arise when you hear the word "easy" or "ease."
2. Write down all the words that arise when you hear the word "hard work."
3. Write about a memory of working hard and how that felt.
4. Write about a memory of something coming very easy and how that felt.
5. Write a plan for yourself, small shifts and changes you can make to infuse your work with ease, kindness and love. For example, take breaks, be light hearted in your work or create with no expectation of a reward.

Day 10: Your Voice is Special and Needs To Be Heard

Yoga brought me back to my voice

I used to sing in high school, but somewhere along the way I silenced myself. While in Kundalini Teacher Training, I began noticing tones that I once heard in my voice as a child. In the Kundalini Yoga practice, chanting and singing are large parts of the class, and they helped me connect to my voice again.

The practice also helped me accept my voice as it is, rather than constantly judging it, trying to make it something other than what it is. As I sang more and more, I realized that the reason I quit singing in the first place was because I'd convinced myself I wasn't good enough.

"Good Enough." I hear this phrase all the time. "I want to sing along, but I have an ugly voice. I'm not good enough." It's amazing that we say these things about our own voices, a gift so precious and unique like a fingerprint. How could a fingerprint ever be bad? It's a fingerprint. A fingerprint is a fact. And just like a fingerprint, the fact of your voice cannot be denied. And if you don't practice using and hearing your voice, you become disconnected from yourself. That's another fact.

Mantra is very effective in helping you connect to your voice. By repeating the same words over and over again, you begin to hear your unique sound and develop a resonance and appreciation for this very primal thing - the sound of your essence. Your voice is good enough. In fact, it's the purest sound ever created.

Meditation *Kundalini

Because this is a Kundalini meditation, it's important to follow the tuning in and tuning out guidelines present in the Introduction Section.

One mantra that is very useful in creating harmony between you and your voice is "Hummee Hum Brahm Hum." It means, "We are we. We are boundless energy (infinity)."

Sit in a comfortable seated position, hands in gyan mudra (thumb tip to index finger tip touching), draw the chin in slightly toward the chest, close the eyes and visualize that you can look at the tip of your nose. Then sing with music, or chant the mantra with no music for 3-11 minutes. You can find the music "Hummee Hum Brahm Hum" in the Resources Section.

Journal Exercise

1. Free write two pages, answering the following questions:

    a. Do I judge the sound of my voice?

    b. How do I feel about the way that I sound?

    c. How long have I felt this way about the sound of my voice?

2. Write the following affirmation 5 times:

> *"My voice carries the vibration of the cosmos. My voice is the sound of my inner universe. When I vibrate love and compassion within, my voice carries the sound of love and compassion. My voice is the sound of love."*

3. Did any thoughts or feelings come up from writing the affirmation?

Day 11: Treat Yourself the Way You Would Like To Be Treated

Yoga helps me learn about projections

I've attended many yoga lectures and the word projection is often used. Up until recently, I didn't quite understand the concept of projection.

I had a big a-ha moment during white tantric yoga in Mexico City. The 62-minute meditation required us to sit across from our partner with our index finger pressed firmly at their third eye point, and they in turn pressed ours. We were instructed to look into our partner's eyes and project positive thoughts toward them.

Sending positive thoughts to a complete stranger was initially a challenge. My thoughts started out as short, positive affirmations in forced, short stutterings "You're beautiful. You are good. You have a sweet heart." And after about thirty minutes of this, the levees broke and erupted rivers of poetry. "You are a beautiful manifestation of the cosmos. The power of your essence is boundless. Your heart is generous, kind, and overflowing with bountiful love!"

Then, something even more interesting happened. My partner's eyes were dark-brown, nearly black like mine. And in an instant I could see the reflection of my face in her eyes. All the things that I was mentally projecting toward her, I was saying to myself! What? It was so beautiful because I realized that most of the time I'm not saying sweet poetry to myself and I could be.

In the processing time following tantric, I grasped that how I treat myself is how I tend to treat others. And I project, paint the picture of my internal landscape, onto the canvas of the people who surround me for better and for worse.

Likewise, through other people's projections onto me, I become representations of someone's mother, friend, sister, or the kid who made fun of them in junior high. And that is where the biggest breakthrough came for me: Other people's projections onto me are not my problem!

At one point I thought it was my responsibility to be liked by everybody or at least make them see that they were projecting onto me. But it's not, and it's not really a big deal. When I see that someone's reaction or opinion is disproportionate to the reality, I just get out of the way. And I've noticed there's less conflict when I allow their opinion to shift or not shift. I just keep on being me! Like Rupaul says, "What other people think of me is none of my god damn business!" Can I get an amen?

Moving forward, I can see that the changes I want to materialize in my life start with me, and how I treat myself. That in turn affects how I treat other people, and sometimes, how I'm treated in return. Instead of only treating others the way you would like to be treated - treat yourself the way you would like others to treat you and see what happens.

Meditation

Sit upright or lie on your back. Set your timer for 3-5 minutes. Begin to say positive things about yourself to yourself. For inspiration, start with the journaling exercise this week and choose some of the affirmations from there; or simply allow positive thoughts to stream through your consciousness and repeat.

Journal Exercise

Today's focus is on self-kindness. In our journaling exercises we'll write personal affirmations to create a nurturing internal landscape.

1. Write twenty nice things about yourself. Where to begin? Start with the simple things that you appreciate about yourself like, "I like the way I smile at strangers," or "I am kind," or "I appreciate life's subtleties." Write quickly and see what comes forward. Use these affirmations for your meditation.

2. Do a little digging. When are the times when you are most hard on yourself? When do you say mean things to yourself. What are your internal triggers?

Use exercise #2 as a road map to discover your self-abuse triggers. The next time you are triggered, breathe deeply and witness your thoughts.

Day 12: Breathe Before You Speak

Yoga teaches me to take a big deep breath before I say something I might regret

You know the feeling right before you send that angry email or say that spiteful comment? I am very familiar with it, and I have said words that caused conflict and even burned bridges.

I've noticed there's a moment, a split-second before I press send or allow the words to pass through my lips when I can take a deep breath and allow the surge of emotion to pass. If I decide to act after that, then I can speak from a place of realness, not crazy emotion or hormones. And when I use this method, half the time I don't even need to speak at all – the situation usually passes or works itself out.

Meditation

Let's explore a long deep breathing practice. To begin, find a comfortable seated posture, or come lying on the back. Notice your breath as you softly breathe in and out through your nose. Notice the rising and lowering of your chest and belly as you breathe in and out.

Notice the simplicity of your breath. Notice it traveling into the lungs, down into the belly.

Inhale to a count of three, exhale to a count of three. Lengthen your breath to a 4 count in and 4 count out.

Practice for 3-5 minutes. This short meditation will help you become familiar with a long deep breath. The next time you feel overwhelmed emotionally, before you speak, access this long, deep breath.

Journal Exercise

1. Write about a time when you said something you wish you would not have said. How did you feel right before you spoke? How did you feel after? Did it make you feel better? Write about every aspect of that situation.

2. So, #1 happened. Now you have the long deep breath to make a different choice next time. Write about scenario #1, except this time imagine yourself taking a breath before speaking or acting. How does this change things? Were you more articulate? Did it cause less harm? Note how taking a pause effects your words and actions.

Day 13: Embrace Your Needs

Yoga teaches me that it's okay to take a nap

My midday naps were once laced with guilt. Aren't naps reserved for the lazy and unmotivated? I was surprised to hear one of my peers in yoga teacher training say the same thing. "I was brought up to work hard and napping is regarded as laziness, so I don't nap," she said.

"Damn" I thought... "I feel like I need naps." I was reading Julie Cameron's *The Artist's Way* at the time, and she validated the need for each person to find a schedule and way of BEing that is right for them. She also said, "Some people will call your idleness laziness, but that is a form of abuse. Giving yourself rest or time to contemplate is not being lazy, it's being aware." And naps are one of the little things I need to do for myself to continue to have the capacity for creativity.

In the past, I've had a tendency toward acting in a way that I intuit makes those around me feel most comfortable, but it's often out of alignment with what I need. Now my yoga and meditation practices support connection with what is nourishing to me in the moment... which is often an afternoon nap!

Meditation

I was given this meditation by a massage therapist who said "This practice is for type-A people. It teaches your muscles how to relax.

Doing this 3-5 times per week provides the physical balance you need for all of your higher frequency activities." Most of us participate in high-intensity activities everyday, so this is a good practice for us all.

Begin by setting your timer for 20-25 minutes. This gives your muscles ample time to release. Lie on your back on the floor and bend your knees at a ninety-degree angle with the knees on a chair or couch. Relax your arms by your side. It's optional to play relaxing music or to place an eye pillow over the eyes. Make yourself as comfortable as possible and relax.

Notice the movement of energy, if any, through your body. Feel yourself softening and letting go of time. When the timer sounds, draw your knees into your chest and rock side-to-side across your spine. Then roll over onto one side and press yourself up.

Journal Exercise

1. Write about a time when you were embarrassed about your personal routines. For instance, maybe you listen to audio to fall asleep and weren't able to do that at a retreat. Or, maybe you wear a certain type of bra because it's more comfortable for you and you had to explain that to someone. Write whatever comes up first.

2. Then write the following affirmation ten times:
It's okay that I _____. This brings me comfort and allows ease in my daily life.

If there's more than one topic, create a new affirmation and write it ten times.

Day 14: There's No Comparison to You

Yoga teaches me not to compare myself to others

I remember when I first began practicing yoga. I looked around the room during each posture to gauge the final shape I was trying to achieve. Mostly I looked to the teachers who seemed to be picturesque in each and every posture.

The turning point came when I found myself in headstand during an Ashtanga class. Though my body fit the shape, I felt extreme discomfort in my neck and shoulders. I was in teacher training at the time and spoke to the lead trainer, who asked me to interlace my fingers behind my head. I could see that my head protruded six inches above my forearms so that my neck received the weight of my entire body when I took a headstand.

The trainer said, "Headstand isn't a good pose for you. Better to work on forearm stand."

I thought, "Great, another thing I can't do!" But over time I saw this as a positive trait, especially as a yoga teacher. Headstand wasn't a good pose for me to do because the physical consequences to my neck outweighed the positive benefits of the pose.

Other teachers and students can practice this posture risk-free, but I cannot. It's really cool that all of us are shaped so differently, inside and out. It's impractical to compare ourselves physically to one another because there are millions of genetic differences between us.

When I teach, I remind students to focus on what they feel rather than the shape of the pose. Even still, I see students look at another person in a pose and mimic their movement or hang their head in shame and disbelief as if to say, "I'll never be able to do that."

Some of us are bendy, so we can take impressive, rock star poses. Some of us have unique physical strengths. For example, I can hold my arms over my head for thirty minutes or more, but I guarantee that does not make an impressive yoga photo, and you'd have to hang around a long time to see it! What a posture looks like on the outside isn't the point of yoga. The transformation of yoga takes place within and manifests itself in subtle ways.

The fruits of yoga are mostly internal with some external side effects. So the next time you practice yoga, focus on feeling rather than shape; because your shape is just beautiful the way it is!

Meditation

In this meditation, we'll focus on looking at ourselves, notice our triggers, and soften around them.

Look at yourself in the mirror. Notice the parts of yourself that you normally criticize (for me it's a scar I recently acquired right between the eyes.) For you, it might be a whole body part.

Look at your place of physical imperfection and allow your thoughts to flow and emotions arise. As they do, continue to look at that spot on your face, that mole or acne scar, that wrinkle, that piece of flesh and begin to conceptualize yourself as a small child, looking in the mirror at that same spot for three breaths.

Then, close your eyes and visualize yourself giving the child-like version of yourself a big hug, embracing yourself as you are in the moment.

The next time you begin comparing and criticizing yourself, do this exercise. Notice the criticism, neutralize it, and see yourself as a child, because who you truly are and what you share is a child-like essence.

Journal Exercise

1. Focus on sensations that arose during the meditation. Free write 1-2 pages.

2. Write about yourself when you were a child. What were some of the unique qualities about yourself that you remember? Focus on the stories and memories that make you chuckle and bring you joy.

During times of comparison or criticism remember yourself as a child with all of your sweetness and innocence.

Day 15: You Are a Gift

Yoga teaches me to embrace my unique essence

When running a business, there are two main approaches. The first approach focuses on competition. You are in competition with anyone who offers your product or service. The second approach focuses on nurturing the qualities of your product that make it one-of-a-kind. With this style of business, the focus is on creating the best version of your product or service possible instead of focusing on the competition.

As a yoga teacher, I can fall into the trap of comparing myself to other teachers – and students also compare. It's a daily practice to remember to stay true to myself as a teacher and share from a space of authenticity. What I offer may look and feel different than the common ideal of what yoga is; but it comes from a place of personal connection to the teachings of yoga, not competition or comparison.

Competition has the by-product of limitation. When we become focused on someone else, we decrease the potential for creativity and spontaneity – the chance to find a voice that echoes a truth forgotten, dormant in our hearts.

There is no need to compete because you are an incomparable, unique essence. Who you are is a gift, not conditional upon how much you make or have in the bank account, who you are or are not dating, what job you have, where you live, what you own, whether you have it figured out or not, or whether you feel like you're progressing or not. All those things are conditional and created by us. The basic fact is you that are here now. The other basic fact is that your unique essence is a gift to all of us.

Meditation

Today's meditation goes deep into conditioning related to competition. In order to connect to the freedom of child-like curiosity, we must get over being better than others. When connected to Spirit, we create out of love and succeed in service of our highest good. Allow lots of processing time after this meditation in order to take detailed notes in the journaling exercise.

Visualize a time when you were in competition and you won. This might be in the arena of sport, a board game, or even a spelling bee. How did it feel to win? Did you feel better than another person? Did you feel pride for all your hard work, indifference, or apathy? Remember the event - the room you were in, the people surrounding you, any nervous or happy sensations. Notice and remember.

Now, visualize a time when you were compared, competed and lost. Remember the moment before you found out, remember what it felt like when it sank in that you had lost. How did you feel? Shame, indifference, apathy?

Hold the two sensations side by side: the sensation of victory and the sensation of failure and experience all the sensations together at the same time. Try not to compare. Hold the feelings of pride and worthiness next to sensations of shame and failure.

Notice that these are both emotions, one not better than the other. Both emotions are rooted in conditioning, yet valuable in the experience. Take three deep breaths to neutralize the emotions and release.

Your success is not conditional on what you have or achieve because at your core your essence is perfect – it is divine.

Journal Exercise

1. Go to a time when you competed or were compared. How did that feel? Write all the sensations associated with winning. Write all the sensations associated with losing.

2. How does the concept of winning or losing effect your choices, i.e., "I would try this but I don't want to be bad at it."

3. How much are you driven by competition versus personal, meaningful growth?

Day 16: We Shape Our Reality With Words

Yoga teaches me to use my voice

Asking for exactly what I need in exchange for a service does not come naturally to me. When it comes to projects fueled by passion, I often ask for too little. But in order to positively shape our environments it's important that we all learn how to express our needs using our words.

As an artist I remember my first forays into booking events and negotiating contracts. I was wont to speak up and ask for travel expenses or a food per diem and ended up spending more money than I made. Now, I don't mind singing or teaching for free a few times, but can't nobody eat for free! I found myself unable to teach or play out as much as I wanted because my energy stores were depleted from lack of basic needs and support.

I've done this in relationships as well, remaining silent instead of communicating in order to avoid anticipated conflict. All the while, I wondered why I was not receiving what I needed while setting the expectation that my partner needed to read my mind.

Not using my voice is rooted in the fear that I will be disliked or shunned for my viewpoint. But, when I don't speak up and express, the silent life that pops up around me is artificial and out of alignment with what I need to do the work I am meant to do.

This makes perfect sense on a basic level. If I don't receive some sort of payment for whatever it is that I do, then I'm unable to cover expenses for food and shelter, and can no longer offer that service.

Likewise, in relationships, if I don't communicate what I want, then I'm in turn expecting the other person to telepathically discover what I'm feeling. Not communicating my needs and desires is really expecting the world to figure out what I want and then getting frustrated and upset when it's not what I want – which is ridiculous!

When my partner and I first started dating, I was astounded by his languaging, "What do you envision for dinner tonight?" he asked. "Wow," I thought, "I've never been asked what I want in this way." Asking what I envision instead of what I want opens me to realize that I have a say in shaping my reality. I make choices and communicate them, then with consistent action, those ideas become a reality; it's as simple as that.

Meditation *Kundalini

Because this is a Kundalini meditation, it's important to follow the tuning in and tuning out guidelines present in the Introduction Section.

Here is a meditation to help you start using your voice. It uses the mantra "Har" which means creative energy. When you chant it, bring the belly button in toward the spine. As you say the word, draw the tongue toward the center of the hard palette for the "r" sound. You can find the music "Tantric Har" in the Resources Section.

Find a comfortable seated position. Place the tips of your fingers directly at the heart center with the fingernails touching and the rest of the fingers curved naturally. The thumbs point upward toward the heart. Close the eyes and focus them at the tip of the nose.

Set your timer for 3, 4, and 5-minute intervals for a total of 12 minutes. Play the music from the resources section in the back, "Tantric Har." For the first 3 minutes chant the mantra "har" out loud. For the second interval of 4 minutes, whisper the mantra "har." For the last 5-minute interval, mentally chant the mantra as you pump the navel in toward your spine and feel the energy of the mantra at your heart beneath your hands. For the final 90 seconds, extend the arms above the head, fingers stretched out wide and chant "har" loudly.

To end the meditation, inhale, hold the breath in, and place the hands into fists and press at the chest. Exhale. Inhale again, hold the breath in, and place the hands into fists and press at the belly below the belly button. Exhale. Inhale for the final time, hold the breath in, and place the hands into fists and press into the shoulders. Exhale and release.

Journal Exercise

1. Write about a time when you wanted to speak, but couldn't because of circumstances or other reasons.

2. What did you want to say?

3. Why couldn't you say it?

4. Close your eyes, take in a deep breath and send your love to yourself in that circumstance.

Writing will help you release the energetic block caused by not expressing what you needed to in the moment. Do this exercise for all the times that you were unable to speak.

Day 17: Notice the Present Moment

Yoga teaches me that most everything is a meditation

When I first started yoga, I practiced Kundalini Yoga most of the time. I loved these classes because at the end, we always practiced a meditation. Sometimes the meditation included singing, weird breathing, and holding my arms in odd positions. I remember holding my arms up one time and feeling like an acupressure point was being pressed. It hurt so bad that it made my stomach hurt. I decided I would put my arms down. At that exact moment the teacher said, "Just a little while longer, hold steady, you're not going to die." Though it felt like I was going to perish at any moment, I held steady through the discomfort, and at the end of the meditation felt a powerful release from the pressure point.

This story reminds me of my return trip from Italy years ago. Very ill, I spent the previous day on the runway before being returned to the terminal due to a starter malfunction. Before taking off the next day another issue arose, delaying the flight further. We finally left the runway after a three-hour delay and flew nine hours westward. I caught a flight to San Antonio from New York and we finally landed in Texas. After fifteen hours of travel, I was ready to lay in bed for at least as many hours when the captain shared this message "Folks, we're about twenty minutes early and don't have a terminal to park in. We'll be here at least another 15 minutes."

I wanted to break down and cry right there. I was so close to the end, so close to home and delayed again! Then I was reminded of the meditation I practiced years ago and the words of my teacher, Liesbet Pryke: "Just a little while longer, hold steady, you're not going to die." I smiled to myself and took a little nap, knowing that my added anxiety wasn't going to make anything move faster. We eventually pulled into the terminal, and I was more rested because I chose to be.

Many circumstances are like this where our patience and discomfort tolerance are tested: being on hold while on the phone with the cable company, waiting in traffic, washing the dishes. In those moments, by moving even deeper in the meditation, we find that sweet space where discomfort melds with ease. We can then reach an appreciation for the temporary state of discomfort that yields to a more pleasurable, open space.

Most things are like this. Most things are meditations.

Meditation

Many times we want to be somewhere that we're not. It's the nature of the mind to imagine some other place that is better than where we are now. This creates conflict in our system in which we become out of alignment with ourselves in the present moment. This meditation helps us to settle into this moment. You can do it several times throughout your day as a check-in.

Set your timer for 5 minutes. Find a comfortable seated posture. Close your eyes and bring your awareness to your breath. Notice how you are breathing naturally without changing your breath. Notice the parts of your body that move naturally with your breath – the flutter of your belly, maybe a light lift through your chest, a slight expansion through your ribs.

Notice your sitting bones pressing down into the earth. Become aware of your tailbone, and the sacrum above your tailbone. Notice your lower lumbar spine with its thick vertebrae and above it, your thoracic spine – the vertebrae getting smaller as they travel upward to the base of your neck. And then the cervical spine getting smaller as it travels up to the base of your head. Notice your head sitting atop your spine.

Soften the base of the tongue. Allow the back molars to part. Maybe even the lips part as you breathe in and out through the nose.

Become aware of the in and the out breath.

Journal Exercise

1. Write 1-2 pages in your journal without lifting the pencil. Free write without any editing. When finished, go back and look at your pages, noticing all the times you write from a cause and effect perspective. For example, I need to go to the grocery store to cook dinner. Notice throughout your day how often you are thinking ahead, preparing for what comes next.

2. Carry your journal with you today and when you notice that you're disconnected from the present moment write down what topics or themes prevail. Note the recurring themes that draw you away from the present moment.

Day 18: You Are Vast. Your Thoughts Are Not.

Yoga teaches me what Bob was talking about

In "Redemption Song," Bob Marley shares that we have the ability to free ourselves from mental slavery, the ability to transcend the story we tell ourselves about ourselves that is at most times a false tale. I encountered such a story during an intense white tantric meditation in 2010. The meditation asked us to extend our arms out shoulder height, toward our partner and make circles around their extended arms then stop as they replicated the motion. We were to do this for 62 minutes.

I remember after about ten minutes feeling extreme discomfort throughout my entire body and that's when I began to hear some internal criticism for considering taking a break.

"C'mon, it's not that bad. Don't be weak." The volume, intensity, and tone of the inner critic increased as the meditation continued, "You always quit. You're not good enough." I felt like I was being terrorized by myself!

It got even worse toward the end when I realized that it wasn't healthy for me to continue. But the internal chatter pushed one more final jab before I released my arms.

"You're a bad person," said the voice. In the middle of the meditation, among 500 people, I released my arms and began sobbing like I've never cried before or since.

The whole tent thought that I was laughing, so everyone erupted in laughter. It was only after a while that the laughs subsided and my sobs sustained that someone said out loud, "She's crying, not laughing." At the end of the meditation, many people came over to hug me or catch a glimpse of the girl who cried so loud it was confused with laughter. I felt exhausted. In the following weeks and months, there was some major processing.

The internal chatter I experienced during the meditation was actually the story I had been telling myself up until that point, ending with the core belief that I didn't feel like I was a good person. I don't know why I formulated that idea about myself – maybe environmental conditioning or something I was mysteriously born with – it was a real component of my consciousness. Looking back at my teenage years, I could see how this core belief led me toward self-destructive choices.

Becoming aware of the story was the first step towards unraveling it. Only then could I create a new reality for myself that embraced my goodness, my sweetness. It doesn't take an intense experience like tantric to learn that about oneself. Just the act of sitting quietly for a few minutes throughout the day to check in and listen to what the mind is saying can be enough to begin unraveling the story.

Meditation *Kundalini

Because this is a Kundalini meditation, it's important to follow the tuning in and tuning out guidelines present in the Introduction Section.

For this Kundalini Yoga experience, let's practice a Kundalini Yoga meditation. This one is to connect with the conscious flow of your essence. I've heard many people talk about having spontaneous spiritual awakenings. Well, this meditation helps you remain stable before, during and after one of these openings.

You can do this meditation sitting up or lying down. Interlace your fingers, the left thumb over the right so that your hands form a sort of cup. Place the heels of your hands at your solar plexus so that there is space between your solar plexus and the interlaced fingers.

Begin a subtle and rapid breath of fire in and out through the nose. Practice this for 3-11 minutes. To end the meditation, inhale and exhale a few times, then sit in silence. Notice the sounds surrounding you.

Journal Exercise

1. Write down a story that you often tell yourself about yourself, like "I'm a bad person. This story comes from the time(s)…"

2. Deny this story. Write yourself a new story. "This story isn't accurate. It may have made sense at one time, but it's bullshit now. Here are the ways that I honor the good in myself." Negate the false story.

Day 19: Be Still

Yoga reminds me that I am whole and complete in this moment

This moment, sitting here, typing this message, is full and realized. It is realized because I dwell in it and recognize its wholeness – nothing more needed to make it better.

I once thought that what made life great is achieving, moving forward, and producing. While I'm grateful for what I have accomplished, I'm most grateful for what I am doing now. I'm in a transition period. I work most days and rest when I'm not working. I haven't had much time to create music or write, yet I'm enjoying where I am.

Instead of wanting to be somewhere else, I understand there's something to learn here. Being present with myself during each moment of this transitory process is a necessary part of the lesson. There has been some criticism from folks (including my inner critic) who want me to produce more, play out more, and teach more; yet, I hear little encouragement for the basics of working and paying bills on time.

To that end, I think the seemingly mundane tasks of everyday life are less glamorous compared to the glories of manifesting big projects and ideas, but both exist and balance one another. I think back to a time when I had to be working on a project in order to feel like I was doing something with my life. I think now for the first time I feel comfortable with where I am and who I've become.

For instance, when I'm asked what I'm up to, the first thing that comes to mind isn't to talk about a project. I'm comfortable saying that I'm working and teaching. Not sure what the end point is. I'm just musing, thinking about how so many of us are so great, just because. No reason or explanation or achievement listing necessary…just because.

Meditation

It's often in the still moments that transition and growth is occurring. Think of the seedling. When you stare at it, it appears that nothing is happening. But step away for even a few hours and you see a shoot poking its head out of the shell. The point is that we don't always see progress or motion, but it is happening. We have to get out of our own way and allow for the movement.

Set your timer for 3 minutes. Lie on your back. Feel the space behind your eyes. Feel the space at the back of the tongue and allow your back molars to part. Notice the back of your head as it rests against the support of the earth. Allow your entire head to rest. Imagine the top, the crown of your head becoming soft. Notice your breath and allow yourself to be here now.

Mentally Repeat:
Spirit runs through me
I am whole

I am complete

I am enough in this moment and this moment is enough

Journal Exercise

1. Do you feel like you need to have something going on in order to feel like you are progressing?

2. Why do you feel or not feel that way? Where does your patterning come from? When you are still, where do you feel it in your body?

3. What does stillness or peace feel like to you? How do you define it?

4. Can you allow yourself to feel worthy while being still? What does that look like in your day-to-day life?

Day 20: Bring Me a Higher Love

Yoga reminds me that all the tools I need are inside of me right now!

This remembering process that I access through yoga and meditation is the definition of love. To know and appreciate my wholeness, that's love, man.

It took me a long time to get out of the cycle of looking outside myself for the next thing that would make me feel that sensation of love. The inward focus of Kundalini Yoga helped me focus on inner expansion of love. Sometimes I felt like I received the sensation of love when I bought a new pair of boots, really nice ones, or when I got attention from this or that person.

But the appreciation of my own inherent awesomeness, based on the foundation that I am flawed, I am human, and I am beautiful, there's nothing more powerful than that. And that love I feel for myself is a fountain overflowing that promotes harmony in all of my environments. Love is a lens through which we can see one another as ourselves, and embrace what is not us as a piece of us.

Meditation

Meditation on Cosmic Love:

Sit upright and set your timer for 5-11 minutes. Feel your whole self in this moment: your breath, your spine, your jaw, your head. Note the sensation of your sitting bones down into the earth.

See yourself where you are located: city, state, country, continent, on planet earth, in the solar system, milky way galaxy which contains millions of solar systems, ours located on the outer spiral. Visualize this galaxy as part of an ever expanding universe, reaching out into infinity.

And with this expansion, the expansion of love and tenderness. Feel yourself as part of this ever expanding capacity for love and understanding.

Bring yourself back. From the cosmos to the milky way to our solar system, to planet earth to your continent, country, state, city, room, into your body. To your tissues, cells, DNA, molecules, atoms, and further still – to the vibrations that form your matter, and visualize an expanding universe within you. Expanding in the capacity for love, awareness and kindness. Dwell in this inner universe. Stay here.

To end, slowly open your eyes with a soft gaze.

Journal Exercise

1. Make a list of self-care actions that help you feel loved and supported. For example, I like to make a facial steam from a pot of hot water and peppermint oil.

2. Choose three things from your list and do them this week.

Day 21: Queefs Happen

Yoga teaches me that it's okay to fart or queef or whatever in public…gas happens!

Yoga not only works on the muscles and bones, but also the tissues, including the organs. On a summer's day in late 2010 during a weekly yoga class, I learned how deeply my vagina was affected by yoga.

As is customary in most Anusara classes, we ended with partner work. My partner, 6'4" & 280 lbs, was to assist me as I floated into a handstand against the wall; and conversely, I was to pray that I didn't get face kicked as he elevated his trunks toward the same wall. He went first and halfway got there after two attempts. With a sweaty brow, he nodded his head in conceit and acknowledgement that it was now my turn to try.

I ascended in the way instructed, making it to the wall upside down quite easily. There I stayed for forty-five seconds or so before deciding it was time to dismount and take a break. That's when it happened.

A full thirty seconds of flatulence emerged from deep within my uterus. As I sat cross-legged, eyes locked with my partner, I tried to shift positions to make this terrible sound stop, but no amount of shifting made a difference, it only shifted the tone. An extended release of old gas sputtered from the recesses of my being with the quaking sound of an old muffler. Humiliation washed over my face, the hot coals of both denial and shame.

But then I thought, "I think this may be as bad as it gets." There's freedom in letting my moola bhanda flap in the wind in front of a complete stranger. All the etiquette and focus on being perceived as lady-like went out the window. It turns out, I'm just another human being who farts like everyone else.

If you fart in class or hear someone else do it, know that it's part of the releasing process of yoga, and it's completely natural. Just don't go around being proud of it – then it becomes a distraction!

Meditation

Chest-to-belly long, deep breath. Set your timer for 5-7 minutes.

Find a comfortable seated position, on your heels or cross-legged. Close your eyes and begin to notice your breath as you breathe in and out through your nose. On the in-breath, draw the breath to your lungs. Notice the expansion of your lungs and ribcage as you breathe in. As you exhale, draw inward and imagine the lungs squeezing in toward your spine.

On your next inhale, draw your breath downward into the belly and notice the slight expansion outward. On the exhale, hug the belly button in toward the spine.

Next, connect the chest to the belly. Inhale, expand through the chest and ribcage, then allow the belly to come out last. On the exhale draw the belly in and the lungs upward.

This long deep breath will help you remain steady when surprises happen. Having the connection to a long deep breath will help you move from a place of reaction to a place of acceptance.

Journal Exercise

Write about a time when you were embarrassed. Then write an imaginary ending, and turn that embarrassment into a funny story.

Extra Credit: Share this embarrassing story with someone! Learn to laugh at yourself!

Day 22: Learn To Listen

Yoga teaches me how to listen…how to really listen

As I've mentioned before, I started yoga with a Kundalini practice. In this type of class, your eyes are closed for most of the time; this requires you to really listen to the teacher in order to follow instructions.

After years of a Kundalini practice, I notice that I've become a better listener. I can close my eyes more often in a Hatha class than I could before. Part of the challenge of yoga is to take cues from a teacher and translate them into my body. This personal challenge offers a deeper understanding of how my body moves.

I remember when this cosmic connection between a teacher and I occurred; when her words were integrated into my body. While in half-moon pose I was directed to move my inner right thigh upward. I heard the instruction, made the tiny shift, and heard her exclaim, "Yes! Good, Robin!" It was a moment between teacher and student where we both understood something deeper than just a physical suggestion was made. I listened and integrated her words into my body – now that's yoga!

As a teacher, I notice how dependent students are on physical cues. I try to demonstrate less, but teaching at studios where the classes are so large and students are so new, it can be a challenge to guide only through vocal cues. If you are new to yoga, or even a long-time practitioner, notice that listening is a huge component of the practice. Decrease your dependence on sight, looking at what the teacher or the person next to you is doing, and try to move your body according to the teacher's instruction. Close your eyes when you can; focus on listening.

This skill of listening will help you outside of the studio. It can even help you hear beyond words to the total message that is being communicated with you. You will become sensitive to tone and notice when words are coming from a genuine place instead of a manipulative one. Listening will teach you to hear the most important voice of all, the voice inside yourself.

Meditation

There is a word in Gurmukhi, called Shuniya. It's pronounced (Shoe-Knee-Yuh). It is a state of indifferentiation or zero point of consciousness where you merge with the whole. The word roughly translates to mean "deep listening." This meditation asks you to say the word shuniya out loud, whisper it, then listen.

Chant Shuniya for 1-3 minutes.

Whisper Shuniya for 1-3 minutes.

Then listen for 3 minutes. Listen to the sounds all around you: the sound of your thoughts; the sound of the traffic; the sound of birds. Listen and invite in all of the pleasant and unpleasant sounds alike. Don't differentiate between good and bad. Bring awareness to all the sounds.

Journal Exercise

Free-write two pages without lifting your pen or pencil. Empty out everything in your brain. Do not censor or differentiate good from bad. Write everything as it flows.

Day 23: Be Gentle With Yourself

Yoga teaches me to appreciate my progress and be patient with my process

Gentleness is a skill much like perseverance. Humans have the unique ability to inflict more pain and suffering on ourselves than any person ever could. I find that I tend to be hard on myself for things beyond my control, like a physical limitation or another person's feelings.

Last year I switched from attending public Kundalini classes to a more gentle, Hatha style. This particular style resonates deeply with me because it allows me to be soft with myself.

I tend to be pretty disciplined, so in the past I gravitated toward yoga practices that reinforced that discipline like Kundalini and Ashtanga. But what I really need is the opposite of my natural tendency, a slow, easeful class that allows me to find pleasure and comfort in my breath and movements. It took me going through a stressful personal relationship to try this slower, more relaxed form. Since then, I've fallen in love with it and myself.

When we're going through stressful situations such as moving into a new home, a new relationship, a fresh break-up, a physical injury, an accident of any type, or caring for a loved one, it's easy to be hard on ourselves to get better, do more, fix things, or put the healing focus on the other. Often, the best thing is to act contrary to the "do more" ideology. When we are overwhelmed and want to act, it's best to "do less," rest, and surround ourselves with softness, comfort, and love.

Meditation

Set your timer for 11 minutes. Sit comfortably or even recline onto the back. Stop. Just stop. If some thoughts come up, follow those thoughts. If you notice a feeling, go with that feeling.

Journal Exercise

1. Write down all the activities that you perform throughout your week from start to finish. Then, sit back and take a look at all that you do.

2. Write down all the goals you have accomplished or are accomplishing right now. Reflect and pat yourself on the back for having done what you intended to do.

3. Investigate. How can you promote more gentleness and ease into your current schedule?

Day 24: Embrace Imperfection and Move Forward

Yoga teaches me to release ambition and relax into intuition

Ambition is a quality that helps us discover new creative pathways, but it must be balanced with intuition. Success and achievement are byproducts of mindfulness, as well as inner love and compassion. For the past six months, I've been riding myself to update my website. It's been a HUGE GLARING ITEM on my to-do list, like the swan hanging from my neck, noose-like and tight. And of course, whatever website I built had to be perfect, nay, more than perfect… remarkable even.

Last week I said F*** IT, I'll let go of finishing it, let go of it being perfect and just play around. And you know what? As soon as I let go of perfection and the goal of completion, I finished it in less than a week. Funny how things like that happen! When I approach tasks with an attitude of play, openness, and intuition, then goals materialize. When I approach tasks as a means for success or perfection, then I get stuck, don't love myself, and miss the point.

Compassion, the befriending of oneself, is the goal. Authenticity, being comfortable in your own skin – that is true success.

Meditation

Set your timer for 3-5 minutes. Place your hands together, palms facing up with the pinky side of your hands touching. Inside your hands imagine a delicate, pink rose. See the rose from an aerial view. Notice the dimensions of the petals. Feel the weight of the bloom in your hands.

Inhale and then sing "Yahm" on the exhale. Yahm is the mantra for the heart chakra. Repeat this until the timer sounds. Take a few breaths feeling yourself connected with this beautiful bloom within your hands. Know that you are a success here in this moment, through your intention of connecting and befriending yourself.

Journal Exercise

Write down 10 actions that a friend performs. A good friend prepares dinner for you and is a good listener; these are both actions. Look at your list once you are done and ask how you might perform these actions for yourself. Like, make yourself a nice dinner and sit in silence to listen to yourself.

Day 25: Keep Good Company

Yoga teaches me to surround myself with people who support my dreams

There's a great saying, "You become the company you keep, so keep good company." When I first heard these words I simultaneously smiled and shuddered.

I smiled because I realized the power I had in choosing relationships that uplifted and supported me. I imagined the characteristics I wanted to embody: integrity, honesty, patience, kindness, prosperity, vulnerability, and the willingness to love and be loved. Then I shuddered because the company I'd chosen for myself was slightly out of alignment with my intentions.

And that's it. We choose who we want close. If I find myself complaining about how this or that person acts, I understand that I choose how much time I spend in their company. It's an empowering act to choose to be alone rather than spend time in the company of those who don't reflect who you are or want to be. When you make space, the right environments and people come around who support your dreams, intuition, and personal growth. It's the alone time that can be the most challenging. But if you give it some time, your good company will arrive.

Meditation

This is a set of moving meditations.

1. Set your timer for 2 minutes. Place your upper arms by your ribcage with your palms facing up and slightly cupped. Begin to make quick backward circles with your hands. Imagine yourself clearing out your space, letting go of old energy and old ways of relating that you would like to see released. Move quickly yet breathe long and deeply.

2. Set your timer for 1.5 minutes. Place your hands in a cup shape. Place the right hand, palm facing down at the level of your throat. Place your left palm facing up in front of your solar plexus. Imagine a big door opening in the physical space between your hands, and you standing in front of the door welcoming new, supportive energy.

To end: release your hands and sit in silence.

Journal Exercise

1. Write about the people in your life. Are they supportive of your personal growth and transformation? If yes, write about how they support and nurture you. If no, move on to the next prompt.

2. Write a letter to the person or group. Tell them what your intentions and goals are. Let them know how they might ideally shift to support you and how their shift will support them in turn.

3. At the end of your letter assess: Will this person be willing to shift into a more loving space, or could I reduce the amount of time I spend with this person to allow space for more supportive company?

Day 26: Let Your Light Shine

Yoga teaches me that it's okay to shine!

I love the quote by Marianne Williamson, "As we let our light shine, we unconsciously give other people permission to do the same."

Hi. I'm Robin. I'm six-foot tall. I've been this way since I was twelve years old. Not only was I tall at a young age, but I was also one of five brown-skinned children in a school of five hundred. It was undeniable that I was different. I tried to balance that external, physical difference by conforming or fitting in with my behavior and denying my inherent uniqueness, thereby dimming my light.

When I say light, I mean the qualities inside each one of us that makes us special, not better, than one another. We're not trying to outshine each other here; but rather, ignite our own internal light and let that be the inspiration through our presence. Through the process we can help someone else to shine their own set of unique qualities and continue to spread the light.

When I first started practicing yoga and meditation, I wore baggy clothes and tied my curly hair back. I wore clothes that allowed me to hide. The physical practice of yoga helped me become comfortable in my own skin, and consequently experiment and play with fitted clothing of different colors and textures. I found a curly-hair specialist, who cut my hair and encouraged me to wear it down. I noticed myself smiling more often. I became familiar and comfortable with shining my light. All of those things are good reasons to try yoga.

Meditation

Set your timer for 3 minutes. Light a candle, one in which you can see the flame. Place the candle 12-24 inches away from your face at eye level. Gaze lightly at the flame. If tears begin to come, allow them to come. Gaze at this light, the representation of your precious, inner light.

To end: Close your eyes and notice that the vision of the flame remains. When you are ready, open your eyes.

Journal Exercise

Write down ten activities that you would like to try…even if they are crazy! Like maybe a hip-hop dance class or the aerial arts. Give yourself permission to try one of these things!

Often, we connect to hidden parts of ourselves by participating in new activities. Sometimes, we don't even know that pieces of ourselves have been obscured by conforming to a schedule that we didn't consciously choose. Yoga, meditation, journaling, and new ways of being activate these parts of ourselves.

Day 27: Intuition Can Be Developed

Yoga teaches me that intuition is a relationship I build with myself

Each time we step onto the mat, we're having a dialogue with our bodies. It's a process of cellular programming. The way in which we move with our breath and the manner in which we practice yoga is very much like how we interact with the world. If our practice is rushed and impersonal, we tend to be rushed and impersonal in our day-to-day lives. When we are patient and mindful with our physical bodies, we learn how to be patient and mindful in our movements and interactions in the world. We learn what feels right and what feels off – when to deepen and lean forward into a posture and when to rest and allow.

When I first began practicing yoga, I looked at what other people did in class and mimicked their body shapes when the instructor gave a cue I didn't quite understand. Likewise, in my personal life, I made choices based on what I saw around me. In short, I looked at others to inform my decisions. But now, yoga is teaching me to look inside for the answers.

And each time I practice yoga and meditation, I'm a different person. My mind is in a new place; my body is a day different; my emotions have shifted from the moment before. Moving with my breath is a way to connect to my inner voice and develop a relationship that I can take out of the studio and use in life.

Intuition isn't something that happens when we master or transcend the body. Intuition is a natural rapport that we build with ourselves through an honest dialogue and a deep relationship with our body. That dialogue is spoken in the language of breath linked with movement.

That's why it's so important to focus on feeling and sensation when we practice yoga versus fitting into a shape, because we are programming ourselves. If we put the intention in our yoga class that we have to fit into a shape to be fully realized, or that we have to suffer in class in order to earn the rewards of savasana, then we take that philosophy into our daily lives. We try to mold ourselves into the ideal worker to earn that promotion or work ourselves to the bone without maintenance or self-care in anticipation of a big break, the big savasana.

But when we practice yoga and meditation with the intention that movement is a gradual awareness-building practice, we cultivate and harvest a loving relationship with our highest self.

Meditation

Set your timer for 5 minutes. Sit in a comfortable seated position and place your hands in a cup shape, palms facing upward at the level of the solar plexus. Imagine a bright orb of light resting in your hands. Inhale, extend the arms out, as if you are offering the orb to someone. On the exhale, bring your arms back in where you began. Use the entire length of your inhale and exhale for the movement.

As you inhale, allow the natural expansion of your lungs to guide the movement of your arms. On the exhale, slowly draw your arms in. This meditation helps to build a relationship between breath and body.

Journal Exercise

We often look around us for comparison and also, inspiration. Let's draw on the inspiration part!

1. Go online and find three people who inspire you. Write down all the reasons they are inspirational.

2. Write down how can you embody their inspirational qualities within yourself, yet still BE yourself.

3. Write down your top three strengths.

Day 28: Learn Self-Trust

Yoga teaches me discernment

So many events and unplanned for circumstances arise in our lifetime that knock us off our feet. Events such as failed relationships, financial setbacks, and other uncomfortable shifts (especially ones we thought would make us happy like a relationship or completion of a project), can make us ask, "Why is this happening? Why did I ask for this? Why didn't I see that sooner?" and tell ourselves, "I could have saved myself a lot of time, suffering, etc."

So from these events and our reactions to them, we can begin to doubt our intuition and lose faith in our inner compass. But it's often not wrong intuition, but the resistance to listening to our inner voice that causes a rift between our dharmic path and autopilot. The cure is mindfulness developed through yoga and meditation.

I think back to college, when I had the opportunity to study at one of the only colleges in the state that offered a music therapy degree plan. My intuition said, "Yes, this is the perfect plan for you." My mind said, "What kind of job would you get with that degree? Better study something with a future, like nutrition."

I listened to my mind and moved forward on a path that didn't feel quite right. And now, after having graduated, I am in a field that utilizes more sound healing than nutrition. I don't regret the path I traveled, yet I recognize that it has been a cycle for me to trust what is of the mind and doubt what is of the heart.

How do we discern what is intuition and what is mind? Intuition is usually the idea that comes without effort, that we try to talk ourselves out of. If the difference between the two is still cloudy, I find that setting an intention around clarity, then sitting in silence with my breath and energy centered in my heart creates some space around the area in question.

So now, I listen and trust my intuition, even if it doesn't make sense to people around me or my rational mind. I honor that important part of myself - the part that took me to my first yoga class, urged me to teach yoga, led me to sing, share and record mantras, and led me to write these words on this page in this moment in time for you to read.

Meditation *Kundalini

Because this is a Kundalini meditation, it's important to follow the tuning in and tuning out guidelines present in the Introduction Section.

This is a Kundalini Meditation for Guidance. Set your timer for 11 minutes. Set the intention on an issue in which you would like guidance. Sit in a comfortable seated position and place your hands in gyan mudra with the index finger touching the thumb on both hands. Then place the pinky side of the hands together with the palms facing upward at the level of your heart center, at the solar plexus also called the xiphoid process. The hands are slightly cupped.

Close the eyes and focus at the tip of the nose with the eyes closed. Repeat this mantra three times on one single breath: "Ong Namo Guru Dayv Namo Guru Dayv Namo Guru Dayvuh." You can find the music "The Complete Adi Mantra" in the Resources Section.

To end, inhale deeply and exhale. Relax.

Journal Exercise

1. Is there a mistake you made in the past that you are beating yourself up about? Write about it. How can you move toward self-forgiveness and compassion toward yourself for that mistake? Can you create a ritual for every time you think of it? Write ten affirmations that help console you when you go to that place of unforgiveness. Maybe it sounds something like: "That relationship with that person hurt me, yet I learned from it and surround myself with comfort and love."

2. Have you ever had an idea or concept that only you understood? How did that feel? Did you feel comfortable sharing it with people around you? When you have an original idea or thought, what do you do with it? Do you share it? If so, with whom? Do you dismiss it as invalid? How do you nurture your original thoughts, emotions, and sensations?

Day 29: You Are the Universe

Yoga teaches me that through all the roles I play and take on, I must remember first that I am a soul. My heart shares the heartbeat of the earth.

After teaching a class, a student said to me, "I feel like you work a lot, Robin." It made me laugh because I'm currently in a transition period where I do work a lot. I notice my ego getting puffed up, "Look how hard I can work. Look how little rest I can get in order to achieve my goals." My own ego is so funny to myself.

In the midst of working, I take on many roles. When I travel into each workplace I shift into another energy portal. Being sensitive, I can be prone to absorbing the identity of the place in which I spend the most time. Also, being prone to wanting to be accepted for doing a good job, I try really hard and morph myself into what I think others want me to be.

It's important to create space between my individual unique purpose and who I am as an essence. I am whole within each moment and what I do in my day-to-day doesn't change my essence.

Your essence is eternal. Your day job is not. Even your creative identity is not what defines you. Who you are is not identified or validated by what music you listen to, who you hang out with, what car you drive, where you work, or even the clothes on your back. Those are all expressions of yourself, but your true self is an essence, much more simple and subtle than all of those identifiers.

Your true self is a soft vibration, a heart connected to the earth's heart and all the hearts of the universe. When you think of yourself in this context, you realize that you are so vast. You are the energy of the universe embodied and expressed in form.

Meditation *Kundalini

Because this is a Kundalini meditation, it's important to follow the tuning in and tuning out guidelines present in the Introduction Section.

Set your timer for 11 minutes. Sit in a comfortable seated position. Place your right hand in your lap. Place your left hand 6 inches in front of your chest, palm facing you. Sing "I am" as you draw the arm in, about 4 inches away from the chest. Then sing "I am" again as you extend the arm out to about 12 inches, palm still facing the chest. Come back to the neutral 6 inches away from the chest and begin the cycle again. Come in close to the chest, then away from the chest, then back to neutral. Continue for the full 11 minutes. You can find the music "I am" in the Resources Section.

To end, inhale deeply. Then exhale, relax.

This meditation acknowledges that you are in the physical form, but you are also larger than your physical body, vast like the cosmos.

Journal Exercise

Picture yourself as a solar system within a galaxy. What are your planets? How many are there? What do they look like? How many moons do each of them have? How many suns or stars do you have? Have fun, be creative, and imagine how to weave your individual characteristics into your own solar system. For example, "I am planet Robin. I have five golden moons. I am one of ten planets circling two stars, etc…"

Day 30: Nourishment Is What You Seek

Yoga teaches me to love myself

This is going to sound cheesy, but I remember when I fell in love with myself. It was after the Sat Nam Rasayan Retreat in Mt. Shasta, CA in 2012. Over the course of a week I camped in a small tent on the side of Mt. Shasta. I left in the early morning for Kundalini and contemplative meditation, and I returned when it was dark to sleep and process the day's meditations.

Many of my habits and issues came up over the week, but the most significant sensation was one of clearing the haze obscuring the view of my inherent sweetness. Like in Shakespeare's *The Tempest*, I had developed the temperament of Caliban, who was called a monster so many times that he eventually became one in mind and physical form. I'd grown up a similar way as Caliban. I was often referred to as a "monster" because of my tenacity on the basketball court and "bad" because of my youthful resistance to conformity. The nicknames formed a neurosis lodged into my system, but these meditations cleared the deception, awakening me to myself.

Have you ever seen something so beautiful, so pure, that there's no question it must be good and right and true? For the first time in my life, I looked in the mirror and saw all those things. I fell in love with myself. I started calling myself "Sweet Robin" when I looked in the mirror.

The fact is that many of us are searching for nourishment in each other instead of doing the work to nourish ourselves. When we are unable to be fully nourished by the other, we project onto them and see all the work that they need to do in order to satisfy our individual needs and desires. Yoga and meditation help us develop the nourishment we seek within ourselves.

This isn't to say that we aren't to take comfort and ease in one another's company, but that the energy of companionship isn't predicated on filling a void within ourselves. The more real we are about ourselves, the deeper and more intimate our relationships become, providing the nourishment that we seek. But if we try to skip a step, and not develop the inner relationship, we'll always be dissatisfied with what other people do or do not provide for us – because we haven't taken the time or the care to provide for ourselves.

When I returned from the retreat, I related to my friends in a completely different way. I noticed myself not grasping or looking for conflict or validation in my friendships. The nature of our conversations shifted and felt more nourishing. And now, I notice that I feel completely satisfied with myself, as I am. This kind of confidence is so powerful and empowering to everyone around you who is willing to see and appreciate it. To some, this confidence is intimidating and off-putting, but that's their problem, not yours.

Meditation

This meditation helps you begin the process of developing self-love and self-appreciation. Set your timer for 5-11 minutes.

Bring the palms together at the center of your heart. Close your eyes and imagine a circle of light around your hands, at the level of the heart. Listen to your favorite version of Om Namah Shivaya and center your breath at the heart. When you are ready, begin to sing along with the recording. You can find the music "Om Namah Shivaya" in the Resources Section.

Journal Exercise

Often what we seek to change in others is what we would like to shift within ourselves. This exercise helps you see where you can begin to make the shift first and see the results.

List your ten common complaints about other people. Do you have any of those same complaints about yourself? Choose one thing that you see both in yourself and other people and write words of encouragement and compassion as you begin to bring awareness to your area of growth.

Day 31: Inspiration Is All Around

Yoga teaches me that there is inspiration to be found in many places - even in Rick Ross!

We were in warrior one, arms in reverse namaste with sweat running down our arms, when cosmically my playlist shuffled to words chanted like mantra, "Eryday I'm hustlin' hustlin', hustlin' hustlin. Eryday I'm hustlin'." I cringed a bit, knowing the following verses contained expletives not fit for a yoga class. And then the class reacted in a completely unexpected way – the entire room resounded in buoyant laughter!

What were once creased brows and tight jaws were now beaming smiles and relaxed faces. Maybe it was the juxtaposition of Desert Dwellers against Ross's big bass vocals or the resonance with the reality of the everyday hustle; but the right song played at the right time and transformed serious energy into universal laughter.

Inspiration is all around us. It's in the song or story on the radio, the hand-wave from our neighbor, the temperature of our surroundings. The art of living is the art of opening ourselves up and embracing the magical inspiration always present around us. Thank you for the inspiration Rick!

Meditation

Set your timer to 5 minutes. Put on a style of music that is waaaaaay outside of your comfort zone. Play that music loud and if you're in a place where you can't listen to music loudly, put your earbuds in. And dance for the whole five minutes. Let go, and let inspiration in!

Journal Exercise

Write about your sources of inspiration. What makes you feel alive and fresh? Can you incorporate some of these vitalizing activities into your daily, weekly, or monthly schedule?

Day 32: Authenticity Heals

Yoga teaches me that PMS is real!

For a long time I denied this reality. There is this time of the month when I move a bit slower, am more sensitive, and get irritated more easily. These are the symptoms of PMS, which differ from female to female for longer or shorter periods of time preceding their monthly cycle.

I was in denial for a long time that the symptoms I felt were indeed a precursor to my cycle. I didn't want to believe that all the clichéd jokes were true – that my feelings and sensations could be boiled down to a simple, "Don't mess with her – it's that time of the month." But when I accepted the truth of this authentic experience, I was able to seek help and heal.

I visited a local Ayurvedic practitioner. Ayurveda is the ancient Hindu art of medicine. I shared my symptoms, and was offered these simple suggestions to follow before my monthly cycle:

1. Get more rest than usual, so shape your schedule so that you can move slower and relax.
2. Practice abhyanga massage
3. Reduce caffeine and sugar intake
4. Drink a few tablespoons of aloe vera juice each day

5. Overall, embrace this time to relax, move slower, and soften

I followed the prescription and had a much more positive experience of my cycle. There was less discomfort and a symbiotic understanding with my body that this is what we do every month. I felt like I could be an ally with myself instead of fighting myself. I could embrace my monthly cycle instead of tolerating it.

But for most of us, there isn't the time or space to slow down. Maybe you have an exam that week. Maybe your child requires more attention. Maybe you're working a bunch.

There is also some guilt for women associated with slowing down, like we are less powerful when we admit to our sensitivity associated with…okay, I'm gonna say it…our period. It's okay to be sensitive and emotional, especially during a time each month when our bodies are saying, "Well, we tried to generate life, but it didn't happen this time. Do-over!" That's a BIG DEAL! Part of realizing the power of the feminine is embracing what we've been told is weakness as strength.

The sooner we get real about it, the sooner we can start supporting each other. I remember I tried to get a sub for my yoga class because I started my period that day and needed to rest. I got a-talkin' to from my boss because being on my period didn't seem like an urgent excuse, not big enough to sub out my class.

Someone else happily stepped in and taught, yet the whole ordeal was insightful. Most of us have been taught to push through the to-do list and most things in life, no matter what. This is a quality coveted in our culture. There are other times when I've expressed sensitivity and my female bosses were more understanding. This made me feel so supported. There is strength in admitting that we need rest, especially during our monthly cycle. I hope we can learn to support each other, both male and female, during our more delicate times.

The remedy for me now is more rest and honesty with the people around me that PMS is real, and I'm goin' through it! PMS is now a reminder to slow down as much as I can and try to be easier and nicer to myself.

Meditation *Kundalini

Because this is a Kundalini meditation, it's important to follow the tuning in and tuning out guidelines present in the Introduction Section.

This meditation is good for soothing the nervous system. Set your timer for 11 minutes. Sit in a comfortable, seated posture. Close the eyes. Curl the tongue and inhale slowly and deeply. At the end of the inhale, press the tongue against the roof of the mouth and form a tight seal. Then, open the mouth wide and exhale out the nose. Repeat by curling the tongue and inhaling through a curled tongue, at the end of the inhale press the tongue to the roof of the mouth until you form a tight seal, then open the mouth wide and exhale out the nose.

To End: When the timer sounds, inhale deeply and retain the breath. Squeeze your whole body inward for a few seconds and then exhale. Repeat this twice more.

Journal Exercise

Identify times when you require more self-care and gentleness. Write yourself a permission letter as a doctor's excuse during your more delicate time. Go back to this letter when you are feeling sensitive or unwell as self-permission to go slow and take time for yourself.

Day 33: The Universe Vibrates

Yoga teaches me that most things are temporary and I can be still and watch the show

Like the dashes that follow a cartoon bee across an animated skyline, circumstances in life fluctuate. Sometimes there is rapid transformation in our families, friends, and culture in general. And other times, life is still and gets boring. In both instances, active and slow, we don't necessarily have to make a change.

My boyfriend and I decided to move in together, and during the planning process I felt deep resistance. It seemed like everything he did annoyed me! I didn't hide it either. I brought up each and every issue as it arose. Underneath it all, I felt a deep love and affection for him, knowing that this move together and our relationship was what I like to call "in-the-flow." But what I wasn't feeling was what I wanted to feel which was the "I-just-met-you vibe."

I was talking with my mentor and she asked how my relationship was going and I told her that I was having difficulty with my boyfriend, but I didn't feel like anything needed to change. She then dropped some real wisdom: "Life moves and we can breathe through it and recognize that's just how things are in the moment," she said.

Later that day I met up with my boyfriend and he gave me a warm hug and a sweet kiss. I smiled, thinking, "This is just how it is right now. And this is damn good." There is a deep pleasure gleaned from recognizing that present circumstances are "just how they are" and we can watch and enjoy the experience.

Meditation

This meditation focuses on the third chakra, our center for character and stability.

Set your timer for 5 minutes. Sit comfortably upright or lie on your back. Visualize a yellow light, like the light of the yellow sun extending from your belly button to your solar plexus. See the yellow light extending in front and behind you, so that the yellow light extends several feet in front of your belly and several feet behind your back. Feel your breath as you inhale and exhale, allowing your inhale to massage your spine and your exhale to extend your yellow light.

To End: When the timer sounds, slowly open your eyes with a soft gaze.

Journal Exercise

Draw your idea of the pathway of life. For instance, when I think about the fluctuations of life, I draw a pendulum. Maybe you think of it more like a parabola or a crazy bit of swirls or something that looks more like a heartbeat monitor. Mark the points of your life when things were crazy and when things got still.

Then draw a long, straight horizontal line through all the fluctuations. Step back and look at your creation. The long line is your essence watching the movement and being completely in it, saying, "Cool; this is happening."

Day 34: Choose Your Target

Yoga teaches me that I have the ability to intentionally direct my focus

A wise teacher once said to me that for every force there is an equal and opposite force. I was offered this advice in the context of success – that I ought to notice when I'm receiving resistance or negative energy from outside forces as a sign that I am expanding in a positive direction. For every force there is an equal and opposite force…it's physics! When we make a personal breakthrough in a new relationship, career, or cycle, some type of resistance tends to come along that dampens our new advancement.

And then we have a choice. We can focus on the haters, hateration, holleration. Or we can intentionally redirect our focus toward all the people, environments, and structures that support our new advancement.

Yoga and meditation have been so helpful to me in this respect. I remember being at a 10-day silent retreat in Kaufman, Texas. As we learned the silent meditation technique, we were directed to scan our body from head to toe, spending extra time on the parts of our body that lacked sensation.

After a while I felt myself intentionally moving my attention to different areas of the body without losing focus. I also felt an awareness of my thoughts. When my thoughts aren't tended to, like an unkempt garden, they become sloppy in their focus. As they move from one thing to the next, they build a story about a person or situation that is far from the truth. But when thoughts are tended to through yoga and meditation, I can intentionally focus on one thing at a time in the present moment.

Meditation

In this meditation, we'll shift our awareness to different areas of our bodies - and try to stay awake!

Come lying onto your back. Set your timer for 15 minutes. Bring your awareness to the top of your head, your forehead, nose, chin, throat, chest, shoulders, elbows, wrists, and fingers. Then shift your awareness to the upper chest, lower chest, belly, hips, front of the thighs, knees, shins, ankles, tops of the feet, and toes. Become aware of the whole front of the body.

Then, bring your awareness to the back of the head, neck, shoulder blades, upper back, lower back, buttocks, back of the thighs, back of the knees, calves, heels, soles of the feet. Bring your awareness to the whole backside of the body.

Then bring your awareness to the entire body and rest there until the timer sounds.

To end: When the timer sounds, slowly awaken through the toes and fingertips. Invite yourself up to a seated position.

Journal Exercise

Write about one dream or project that you would like to see manifested. Focus on that one thing and write about all facets of it. What does the end look like? Write down each step leading toward your vision.

Day 35: Set an Intention

Yoga teaches me the importance of intention

In the beginning of each yoga class, we are often asked to set an intention. I wondered about the true meaning of intention for a long time. Is it something that I want to happen? Is it something I am using my will to make happen? How do I set it and what do I choose?

I've noticed over time that the concept of intention is the first step in setting my focus and awareness. My focus goes where I set my intentions. And in that way, intentions are manifested into reality. It's not a super cosmic thing, though when it happens it can feel that way. It's a very practical thing. I like to follow these three guidelines for setting intentions:

First, state what it is you are working with. We are all working on something – patience, compassion, jealousy, working through various habits, etc. Be real and state what you would like to see transformed.

Next, ask for help. We all need help and support. In this step, ask for help from an energy source that you deeply connect with. Maybe it's your higher self, a deity of some type, or simply the energy of the universe. The most important part is that you believe and feel supported by this energy source. "_____, help me as I become more compassionate." "_____, take this negative energy away from my life and infuse my environment with peace." Whatever your intention is, ask for help and support in seeing it resolved.

Finally, state what you will do in the physical world to make your intention happen. If you are working on taking better care of your body, you can say, "I will walk fifty minutes today." Set your sights on what you can do to make the intention real through the day and honor it. It can be big or small…there is no action too small to help your intention be realized.

On most days before I get out of bed, before I do my daily meditation, or before teaching, I set this 3-part intention. It makes so much sense to first set the focus, secondly call upon energy outside, and finally acknowledge the energy within to create change and transformation. If you work with the same intention daily and stick to what you say you'll do to make the intention happen in the third step, you'll be amazed at the results.

Meditation

Today, begin with the journal exercise. After completing the exercise, rest the paper in front of you. If you're writing directly into a journal, then place it open-faced in front of you.

Find a comfortable seated position and set your timer for 7 minutes. Close your eyes and mentally work through what you wrote, your three-part intention. Then place your hands in the shape of a cup in front of your heart and imagine yourself holding your intention in your hands. This is a neutral position because you are offering your intention to the support of all things and at the same time grounding in the physical awareness of actions you have to take to see it made real. Sit here with eyes closed and feel the weight of your intention in your hands, balanced in the mystical and the physical, both in the present moment.

To End: When the timer sounds imagine handing your intention off to your cosmic deity and release the position.

Journal Exercise

Write the following phrases out and fill in the blanks:

1. Today I would like to see progress made in _____.
   (short intention)

2. I ask for the support of _____ (deity or cosmic guide) to help me see, feel and experience movement with _____ . (intention)

3. Today I will _____ (action that you can do today) to help my intention come to fruition.

Now, move on to the daily meditation.

Day 36: We All Got Issues To Deal With

Yoga teaches me to look at my shit and be okay with it

We're always gonna have issues, or as one of my favorite teachers refers to as, "shit." These main themes in our lives emerge as cycles, pointing to us saying, "Here is an opportunity to learn and grow." She also said something I will always remember. As we waded through the waves on the beaches of Tulum, Mexico she said, "The shit will always be there. We'll just get different perspectives as we circle around it over time."

In my mind I envisioned a labyrinth with poo in the center. Sometimes I see it up close, sometimes from far away. I also see it from different perspectives, with the light from the east, sometimes from the west. And sometimes I even turn my back to it, knowing it's there by smell, and also knowing I've tended to it enough so that it's not increasing in girth.

"The shits" are recurring patterns or cycles that emerge from time to time. If we're aware enough, we can recognize that our situation has probably happened before under different circumstances. We may think, "Why is this always happening to me?" Well, often our attention and focus create or draw the cycles to us. Each time, we have the opportunity to see the patterns from a different perspective. When we work through the pattern in a way that feels nourishing and sustainable, the pattern won't emerge as often or as intensely in the future.

These recurring patterns can become problematic when they aren't looked at and tended to regularly. This is where yoga and meditation come in. They are the salve on the wound showing us the end and beginning of a cycle, and how to better navigate both inner and outer conflict. The result is better boundaries and fewer burned bridges. There are thousands of meditations available to you. Pick one. And do that one.

It's so simple. Pick a meditation, do it everyday, see your shit in the light, start the process of release and be free from moving from drama to drama. The difference between history and baggage is that history is an issue recognized and processed, baggage is an unprocessed history that inhibits us from moving forward in life and accessing what we truly want. I don't know about you, but I don't wanna be no bag lady.

Meditation

Today's meditation helps us see the reality of a situation. With perspective, we can work through the cycle rather than dramatize it.

Set your timer for 5 minutes. Find a comfortable seated position. Rest your hands in your lap and we'll practice the mantra "Hrim." Pronounced "H-reem." Hrim is a bij or seed mantra that helps you see what's really goin' on. It's a mantra for clarity. We'll practice the mantra quickly with each repetition of the word lasting a bit more than one second.

To End: When the timer sounds, take a deep breath in, retain it, then exhale. Sit for a few moments in silence and notice how you feel. Take as long as you'd like.

Journal Exercise

For fun we'll do a drawing exercise. Draw a big pile of stuff in the center of your piece of paper and name it. Maybe it's "abandonment" or "stubbornness" or "fear of commitment." Name your poo! We all got it; it's okay!

Then, draw a spiral around it. The spiral starts out up close and then circles out and around the center.

Along the spiral, write three or four action items that support the "flushing" or releasing of this center item. They could be big or small actions.

Day 37: It Doesn't Have to Be So Hard All the Time

Yoga teaches me to follow my bliss

I once thought that in order for something to be effective, it had to be hard. Many of us feel the rush of pushing past our perceived threshold to new areas of physical experience. It makes us feel empowered to overcome a challenge.

But there is a balance in all things, and there is an equal empowerment available to us when we allow ourselves to be at ease. I remember when a teacher gave me permission to find ease in my movement. "What a concept," I thought, "I'm going to try a little less and relax more." A rush of endorphins flowed through my veins, a soft warmth and vitality I'd never felt. My nervous system had received valuable information: "It's okay to soften," and it responded with a pleasant sense of ease. "This is bliss." I thought.

In yoga class we are programming our cells, teaching them how to respond to stimuli once we leave the mat and step into the world. When I started to practice ease in my movements and allowed for softness, my everyday life presented the ease I'd embraced in my yoga practice.

Following my bliss means following the effortless flow of conscious ease. It's not easy to follow, quite the opposite. Sometimes, I'm convinced that in order for a project to be fruitful, it needs to be work, it needs to be challenging, but this is not true. I'm still faced with challenges, but I breathe into them, lean into them, love into them, smile into them, until they release and soften. This is the path of pleasure, the path of ease, the path of following your bliss.

Meditation

Today we'll practice a mantra that connects with our "pleasure body." That mantra is "Ang Sang Wahe Guru." Pronounced "Ung Sung Wah-Hay Goo-Roo." This mantra means: "The dynamic, loving energy of the Infinite Source of All is dancing within my every cell, and is present in my every limb."

Set your timer for 5 minutes and find a comfortable seat. Begin to repeat the mantra in a speaking voice or even singing voice, "Ang Sang Wahe Guru." You can find music to this mantra in the Resources Section.

To end: Picture a light blue aura of light surrounding you in all directions. Rest in this light for as long as you would like.

Journal Exercise

Today we'll journal in a new physical environment – at the park, a coffee shop, on your sofa. The possibilities are endless. Free write two pages about how your physical surroundings change the way you feel. Keep the pen connected to paper the whole time. If you're typing, continue to type without pause.

Day 38: Moving on Is a Skill

Yoga teaches me to let go and move on

Aparigraha is a Sanskrit word meaning non-possessiveness. It's one of the yamas in the eight-limbed path of yoga outlined in the yoga sutras by Patanjali. The practice of aparigraha basically means clearing space by letting go of the old in order for new, fresh energy to flow. This brings lightness and vitality into our lives. It can be overwhelming to hear that we have the power to let go of grudges, perceived injustices, and painful past events.

It can be more comfortable to be the person who is on the receiving end of an action. "This thing happened to me, therefore I am _____" But, like the wise poet Rakim said, "It ain't where you're from, it's where you're at." It's a way of saying that what happened to us in the past doesn't define our future. It undoubtedly shapes us, but we can use those experiences as momentum to birth into a new, elevated understanding of ourselves. We can leave the parts behind that no longer serve us and keep the parts that truly teach us.

It's like housecleaning. You know that light feeling you get when you've thrown away the excess, let go of some old clothing lingering in the closet, maybe even some receipts with no home or purpose? You get that feeling because clearing the clutter creates ease and a free flow of energy in your home that promotes harmony.

It's the same with letting go of grudges, forgiving the people who harmed you, forgiving yourself for any harm you've intentionally or unintentionally caused others, and taking really good care of yourself. Aparigraha is a practice of internal housecleaning and we gain perspective as events unfold in life when we use yoga and meditation. Yoga brings the focus to ourselves and helps us find solutions and insight based on our own actions. It changes the story from, "This thing happened to me; therefore, I am that," to, "This thing happened to me; I can see where it came from, and next time I can try responding in a new way. It's not the end of the world, I can let it go and move on." Big difference!

Meditation *Kundalini

Because this is a Kundalini meditation, it's important to follow the tuning in and tuning out guidelines present in the Introduction Section.

This meditation is also called the "Prosperity Meditation." It helps activate your naval center so that you can clear out all the crap, making room for new energy. You can find the music "Tantric Har" in the resources section.

Set your timer for 3-11 minutes. Place the index finger side of the hands together, palms face down. The thumbs cross as you knock the sides of the index fingers together. As they collide, the thumbs cross. Allow the right thumb to slide below the left thumb. As you do this, chant "Har." Then, bump the pinky sides of your fingers together with the palms facing upward and chant "Har" again. Keep doing this at a pace of one "bump" per second.

To End: Inhale deeply, retain the breath and release. Do this a total of three times.

Journal Exercise

Clearing out the energetic closet. Who are you holding a grudge against? Who hurt you so much that you haven't forgotten? Write a letter to that person you want to forgive. Tell them what they did that hurt you and how it affected you and why. Find a fire-friendly receptacle, go outside and burn the letter. As you burn the letter say, "I forgive you and I forgive myself for the parts we played in this interaction. I'm releasing my grudge against you and freeing myself at the same time."

Day 39: There's Still More Room To Grow

Yoga teaches me to set clearer boundaries

Before I began practicing yoga, I had frequent grand mal seizures that occurred in public spaces with large groups of people. As a result, I stopped going to see live music or attend large public events. I formed the mental relationship, people equals bad. When I started practicing yoga, I began to notice that I'm a pretty sensitive person who tends to take on the prevailing energy of a room. If someone is in a bad mood around me I don't just feel it, I become it.

Yoga and meditation helped me to see that it's not my responsibility to take on another person's mood and that I can set better energetic boundaries. When I notice I'm taking on a sensation that doesn't belong to me, I make a conscious decision not to take it in. I say to myself, "This is coming from so-and-so, and it's not my issue to fix, process, or take on."

I've experimented with setting better energetic boundaries when I'm in big groups. When I feel a wave of energy coming on, I imagine a long line of energy coming from the universe down into the crown of my head, through my body, through my feet, and back down into infinite space. Then, I imagine a warm orb of light surrounding me, and then a blank screen. I've been doing this for years and it helps me feel grounded.

It's been over ten years since I've had a seizure. The exact cause is still unknown, though I feel my recovery is directly related to reduced stress levels I've been able to achieve through yoga and meditation, balanced diet, and adequate sleep.

Austin City Limits, ACL, is a personal yardstick for my crowd tolerance. ACL is a large music festival with upward of 50,000 people. The last time I attended ACL was in 2005. I was so unsure of myself then, nervous about how I would respond to the large group. I had my last seizure in 2002, and ACL 2005 was a huge test. I walked in with two good friends who held my hand because I was so frightened and overwhelmed by the crowd. I managed to get through the day, but it wasn't fun, it was endured.

I reached a personal milestone when I attended ACL 2014. It was the first time I was able to open up and just enjoy myself in a crowd that big. I feel like yoga and meditation have strengthened my nervous system so much, I was just able to be there and have a good time like a normal person! It was a deep personal victory for me.

Yoga helps us set more concrete boundaries, in addition to energetic ones. It helps us see what works for us and what doesn't, the difference between flexibility and deference, wisdom and bull doody, so we can make subtle shifts that positively shape our daily environment.

Meditation *Kundalini

Because this is a Kundalini meditation, it's important to follow the tuning in and tuning out guidelines present in the Introduction Section.

This meditation helps to clear the heart center and balance the nervous system. Set your timer for 3-11 minutes. Place the hands together at the heart center, palm to palm. Inhale in four sniffs, each one lasting about one second. At the end of the four-segments your lungs are completely full. Then exhale in four segments. At the end of the exhale, your lungs are completely empty.

To end: Inhale deeply, retain the breath and release. Do this a total of three times.

Journal Exercise

1. Write about a time when somebody else's energy affected you. How did that feel? Is there a particular energy, like anger or joy, that you are particularly sensitive to?

2. Write down a personal ritual that you can do each time you are taken over by another person's mood. Maybe you wash your hair or create a personal affirmation such as, "It's not my responsibility to take on this energy." Allow the ritual to be personal and meaningful.

Day 40: It's All About the Journey

Yoga teaches me that almost is enough

In everyday life, we set goals. Sometimes the manifestation of them takes a different path from the one that we envision. That's okay – that's the point actually. It's a freeing thought that we don't control every little detail that unfolds in our day-to-day lives. We set intentions, do the work, and see the results unfold.

When I released my third album, *The Essence*, I thought that it would be an instant success. However, things didn't unfold how I intended. The album didn't receive the big splash that I thought it would, that I felt it deserved and was disappointed. I suffered through a kind of creative postpartum depression, disconnected from my artistic creation because I felt like it wasn't being listened to or understood. Also, the project went way over budget, so I ended up in debt.

Still coming out of this debt the following summer, I didn't attend summer solstice for financial reasons. I was bummed because I really needed the inspiration and wanted to be with my yoga community. Still in Texas during the festival, I received a text from a close friend telling me that after white tantric they played a song from my album several times and it made so many people happy!

That made me feel great! I intended or thought that this kind of reception would take place a year earlier. But that's how things unfold, in a direction that we intend, on a path that's unpredictable. We have to trust that the work we do is enough, and then let it go, sit back, and watch our work become visible.

I received some good advice from a wise lady recently: "Don't ever give up, but do slow the fuck down!" And sometimes we need to remind each other of that. We do a lot. Less is more, and we each move at our own pace – and that's beautiful. As long as we keep trying, who cares how long it takes.

Yoga's taught me that. As a teacher, I watch people move into different shapes, each body so unique and different, flowing and breathing at its own pace. I've been injured and had to start all over again, adapting my pain-filled body into child's pose for most of class. And in some classes I've felt like a badass, taking on shapes that felt and looked goddess-like.

On the days we don't make it or don't feel good enough, and we all know what that feels like, we can remind ourselves that almost is enough and let go of the extra judgment and shame for not being perfect or for falling short of our goal. The achievement is in the trying, taking risks when our intuition calls us, and staying committed to our calling.

Thank you for listening and your encouragement. Sharing my life with you in this way has facilitated a big heart opening and I hope there is some resonance in here for you, too. Above all, I hope my stories encourage you to build your own yoga, meditation, or other ritual practice that reminds you that you are so special and precious.

When we love and honor ourselves in this way, it creates a spark that I believe can change the world, beginning with our little world first. The way out is in, and I believe it because I've experienced it. I want you to have an experience of yourself too. That is my intention for sharing these tools to support your self-discovery.

Meditation

Set your timer for 11 minutes. Sit in a comfortable seated position. This is a mantra meditation. It pays homage to the everlasting essence within you…the sense of inner space. The mantra is "ad guray nameh, jugad guray nameh, sat guray nameh, siri guru dayvay nameh." As you chant it, imagine a translucent purple light surrounding you in all directions. You can find the music for this mantra in the Resources Section.

Journal Exercise

Gratitude Journal. It's a powerful practice to do this everyday for 40 days.

1. Write down three things that you are grateful for.

2. Write down three things that would make this day magical.

3. Write down three things about yourself, in the form of "I am _____" that make you feel powerful and strong.

Closing...Day 41

Yoga teaches me that gratitude is a force that nurtures all my environments

I had a meditational experience recently that helped me see what "juice" was missing from my life, and that's gratitude. So often, I only focus on what can be improved or fixed, and then I miss all the blessings present in my life. In this recent meditation, we focused on being thankful for all the structures and people who enrich our lives.

Since then, before each meal, I take time to thank our majestic synergy with the earth. It is a miracle how what comes from the earth meshes with us, providing both fuel and raw materials for our cells. I thank the earth, the food, those who helped cultivate it, my present company, the ability to provide food for myself and my family, my body, the ability to walk, speak, communicate and create, the planet, nature, the breath.

It is enriching and nourishing to share and express pure gratitude. Thank you for your sweetness. Thank you for reading. Thank you for your sincere practice and the courage to be vulnerable and investigate the realms of Spirit and heart. Thank you.

Resources

1. Page 19 Ocean Sounds, "Sleep Waves," by CalmSound
2. Page 30 "Hummee Hum Brahm Hum," by Dharampal, *Power in Peace*
3. Page 48 "Tantric Har," by Simran Kaur Khalsa
4. Page 82 "Complete Adi Mantra," by Dharampal, *The Mantra Project*
5. Page 84 "I am", by Sat Kartar, *Listen*
6. Page 88 "Om Namah Shivaya," by Dharampal, *The Essence*
7. Page 108 "Ang Sang Wahe Guru," by Jai Kartar, *Golden*
8. Page 118 "Aad Guray Nameh" by Snatam Kaur, *Prem*

Bibliography

1. Cameron, Julie. *The Artist's Way*. New York: Jeremy P. Tarcher/Putnam, 1992. Print.
2. Williamson, Marianne. *A Return To Love: Reflections on the Principles of A Course in Miracles*. New York: HarperCollins, 1993. Print.

www.ingramcontent.com/pod-product-compliance
Lightning Source LLC
LaVergne TN
LVHW061225060426
835509LV00012B/1424